THE FAMILY FLAVOR

125 Practical Recipes For
the Simple & Delicious

By Whitney L. Ingram
Photography by Sheena Jibson

THE FAMILY FLAVOR:
125 Practical Recipes For The Simple And Delicious

Whitney Ingram

GhostWest, LLC 780 Smithridge Drive #200 Reno, Nevada 89502
Email: Info@Ghostwest.com

ghostwest.com

Photography by Sheena Jibson

Compiled and Formatted by: GhostWest, LLC

ISBN-10: 1484884043

ISBN-13: 978-1484884041

Printed in the United States of America

Contents

7   *Introduction*

9   *Chicken & Turkey*

35   *Beef*

57   *Pork*

75   *Seafood*

97   *Vegetarian*

119   *Pasta & Polenta*

135   *Soups*

153   *Salads & Dressings*

167   *Sides*

191   *Bread*

201   *Desserts*

243   *Drinks*

248   *About the Author*

249   *Thanks*

Introduction

Why call this book "The Family Flavor"? Because when it comes down to it, everyone's favorite memories repeatedly involve family and food. Think about it: Sitting around the table together, enjoying a Sunday roast with mashed potatoes and drowned in gravy. Tiny little hands helping roll some biscuits to be baked and covered in sticky sweet jam. Big chocolate birthday cakes with colorful candles. Outside enjoying dinner, piping hot off the grill. Food is what connects all of us. It's what we all have in common. The most important things we can do as parents can happen around a dinner table, so we might as well make it taste good.

Feeding my family brings me the most joy. Whether it's being able to satisfy a random craving or provide nourishment on a weeknight, the happiness I feel when I watch my favorite people savor something that I made just for them cannot be calculated. I feel the full measure of motherhood when I can nurture my family through food. My hope is that you too will find that joy. May these recipes encourage and enlighten you.

I dedicate "The Family Flavor" to you and your family and the meals you enjoy together.

Chicken & Turkey

Sun-Dried Tomato & Pine Nut Stuffed Chicken 11

Oven-Fried Chicken 12

Turkey Sloppy Joes 15

Grilled Chicken Quesadillas with Chile Pepper Spread 16

Cheesy Chicken & Rice 19

Michelle's Sweet Soy Chicken & Rice 20

Slow-Cooker Tomato Basil Chicken 23

Sesame Udon Noodles with Chicken & Broccoli 24

Honey Almond-Glazed Chicken 27

Braised Chicken with Mushrooms & Red Onions 28

Curry & Yogurt Roast Chicken 31

Sesame Ginger Turkey Sliders 32

Sun-Dried Tomato & Pine Nut Stuffed Chicken

This is something that I like to make for dinner guests. It looks so pretty and impressive. The chicken can be stuffed ahead of time, only needing a quick searing and baking before dinner. People adore this stuff: melty mozzarella, tangy tomatoes and pine nuts. Everyone loves pine nuts. You are lame if you don't like pine nuts.

Yields 6 Servings

6 boneless, skinless chicken breasts

3 cups shredded mozzarella cheese

¾ cup diced sun-dried tomatoes

½ cup pine nuts

2 teaspoons dried basil

1 teaspoon kosher salt

1 teaspoon ground pepper

Kosher salt and ground pepper, for seasoning

2 tablespoons extra virgin olive oil

Preheat oven to 400 degrees F.
Spray a baking sheet with non-stick spray and set aside.

Put one chicken breast inside of a zip top bag. Seal the bag. With a meat mallet, pound out the chicken breast until about a ¼ inch thick. Repeat with the remaining chicken breasts.

In a medium bowl, combine mozzarella, tomatoes, pine nuts, dried basil, salt and pepper. Mix well to combine. Scoop ½ cup of the mozzarella mixture onto the center of a pounded chicken breast and spread evenly. Roll up the chicken breast, tucking the mozzarella mixture inside. Secure the ends with a few toothpicks. Season all sides with salt and pepper. Set aside on a plate. Repeat with the remaining chicken breasts.

In a large skillet over medium high heat, add olive oil. Once the oil is heated, add three of the stuffed chicken breasts. Sear on all sides, but not cooking all the way through. Set onto the prepared baking sheet. Repeat with the remaining stuffed chicken breasts.

Bake the stuffed chicken breasts for 15-20 minutes, or until an inserted thermometer reads 165 degrees F. Carefully remove the toothpicks before serving.

Oven-Fried Chicken

Have you ever had truly great fried chicken? Besides the crispy skin and moist meat, did you enjoy the calories? What about the greasy fat content? Pretty delicious? This chicken can give you a lot of the crispy, moist goodness minus the deep fry. Corn flake cereal makes up the crispy crust and a couple of dried herbs get mixed in to add flavor. This chicken is not only great for a group, but also an excellent alternative to the deep frying mess.

Yields 6 servings.

3 cups corn flake cereal

1½ teaspoons kosher salt

½ teaspoon ground pepper

1 teaspoon dried basil

1 teaspoon dried oregano

1 teaspoon dried thyme

½ teaspoon garlic powder

⅛ teaspoon crushed red pepper flakes

2 eggs

¼ cup milk

8 bone-in chicken legs, thighs or both

Preheat oven to 450 degrees F. Spray a baking sheet with non-stick spray and set aside.

In the bowl of a food processor, combine corn flake cereal, salt, pepper, basil, oregano, thyme, garlic powder and red pepper flakes. Process until corn flakes are coarse crumbs. Pour corn flake crumbs into a shallow dish, like a pie plate, and set aside. In another shallow dish, combine eggs and milk. Whisk until well combined. Set aside.

Set up a breading station. In order, line up chicken, egg mixture, corn flake crumb mixture and prepared baking sheet. With one piece at a time, dip the chicken in the egg, then into the crumb mixture, coating well, and then onto the baking sheet. Repeat until all chicken is breaded.

Bake for 45-50 minutes or until an inserted thermometer reaches 165 degrees F.

Oven-Fried Chicken
Cucumber Tomato Salad with Lemon & Dill, Pg. 163

Turkey Sloppy Joes

Not your regular sloppy joes. Instead of beef, here we have turkey, packed with protein and not with fat. Besides lots of turkey, there are also plenty of vegetables for a substantial, nutritious punch. When I think of sloppy joes, the teenager in me can't help but think of the crazy lunch lady in "Billy Madison". "Have some more shloppy joes! I made 'em extra shloppy for you! I know how you kids like 'em extra shloppy!"

Yields 6 servings.

1 8-ounce can tomato sauce

2 tablespoons brown sugar

1 tablespoon dijon mustard

1 teaspoon apple cider vinegar

1 teaspoon worcestershire sauce

2 tablespoons extra virgin olive oil

1 celery stalk, diced

1 green bell pepper, diced

½ yellow onion, diced

2 garlic cloves, minced

1½ teaspoons kosher salt

½ teaspoon ground pepper

1 pound ground turkey breast

6 hamburger buns

In a medium bowl, combine tomato sauce, brown sugar, dijon mustard, vinegar and worcestershire sauce. Whisk well to combine and set aside.

In a large skillet over medium-high heat, add olive oil. Once the oil is heated, add the celery, green bell pepper, onion, garlic, salt and pepper. Saute until the vegetables are softened, about 10 minutes. Add ground turkey. Break up the turkey with a wooden spoon and stir occasionally until cooked through, about 5 minutes. Add tomato sauce mixture and stir well. Reduce heat to medium and simmer for 5 minutes, until the sloppy joe mixture is well combined and liquid is reduced. Serve a big spoonful on each hamburger bun.

Grilled Chicken Quesadillas with Chile Pepper Spread

I have a confession. I do not like cheese. I know, right now you are astonished and getting ready to close this book. But I should also confess that I really like these quesadillas, cheese and all. Maybe it's the subtle heat from the chiles or the charred tortilla. Whatever it is, these quesadillas make me a temporary cheese lover.

Yields 6 servings

3 boneless, skinless chicken breasts

Extra virgin olive oil, for seasoning

Kosher salt and ground pepper, for seasoning

2 tablespoons extra virgin olive oil

1 poblano chile, seeded and roughly chopped

1 anaheim chile, seeded and roughly chopped

½ red onion, roughly chopped

½ teaspoon kosher salt

2 garlic cloves, minced

1 chipotle pepper in adobo sauce, seeded

2 cups shredded cheddar cheese

2 cups shredded Monterey Jack cheese

12 flour tortillas

Preheat oven to 400 degrees F.

Place chicken breasts on a baking sheet. Rub a small amount of olive oil onto each one and season each with salt and pepper. Roast for 25-30 minutes, or until an inserted thermometer reaches 165 degrees F. Allow to cool, shred into bite-sized pieces and set aside.

In a medium skillet over medium-high heat, add 2 tablespoons olive oil. Once the oil is heated, add the chiles, red onion and salt. Cook until softened, about 5 minutes. Add garlic and saute for 1 additional minute. Remove pan from heat and pour chiles and onions into the bowl of a food processor. Add chipotle pepper. Process until smooth. Transfer spread to a small bowl.

Set grill to medium-high. To assemble quesadillas, spread a thin layer of chile pepper spread on one side of two tortillas. On one tortilla, on the side with spread, add a little of both cheeses and a small handful of chicken, spread evenly. Top with the other tortilla, spread side down. Carefully grill the quesadilla until the cheese is melted and the tortilla is crisp, 3-5 minutes on each side. Remove from grill, cut into triangles and set on a serving platter. Repeat with the rest of the tortillas.

Cheesy Chicken & Rice

This is comfort food 'round these parts. Gooey, cheesy rice with chunks of chicken. My oldest child especially loves this. If I ever ask him what I should put on our week's dinner menu, he always says "That one cheesy chickeny rice stuff." Said like a true 7-year-old.

Yields 8 servings

3 boneless, skinless chicken breasts

Extra virgin olive oil, for seasoning

Kosher salt and ground pepper, for seasoning

4 cups low-sodium chicken stock

2 cups long grain white rice

¼ cup unsalted butter

½ yellow onion, diced

1 teaspoon kosher salt

½ teaspoon ground pepper

2 garlic cloves, minced

½ cup heavy cream

½ cup chopped sun-dried tomatoes

2 tablespoons minced fresh parsley

2½ cups shredded cheddar cheese

Preheat oven to 400 degrees F. Set chicken breasts on a baking sheet. Rub a small amount of olive oil onto each one and season with salt and pepper. Roast for 25-30 minutes, or until an inserted thermometer reaches 165 degrees F. Allow to cool, chop into bite-sized pieces and set aside.

While the chicken bakes, prepare the rice. In a medium saucepan over high heat, add chicken stock. Once boiling, stir in rice, cover and set heat to low. Simmer for 15 minutes and then stir, cover and cook for an additional 5 minutes. Remove pan from the heat, fluff rice with a fork and set aside.

Heat broiler to high. In a large skillet over medium heat, add butter. Once butter is melted, add onion, salt and pepper. Saute until onion is softened, about 10 minutes. Add garlic and saute for an additional minute. Increase heat to medium-high and stir in chicken, heavy cream, sun-dried tomatoes and parsley. Stir well, then add rice and 1½ cups of the cheese. Stir until cheese is melted, about 3 minutes. Transfer rice mixture to a 9x13 inch pan, sprinkle remaining cheese over the top and set in broiler until cheese is melted, about 3 minutes.

Michelle's Sweet Soy Chicken & Rice
Recipe by Michelle Hall

Someday I should write Michelle a thank you note. It would say, "Thank you for this recipe. It is the go-to recipe around this house. Everyone loves it! I can feed my hungry brood in the time it takes to cook rice and even have leftovers for lunch the next day. You have saved us! Thank you again!" Hopefully Michelle, my sister's mother-in-law, reads this. This chicken and rice is perfection. Chicken simply sauteed and then covered in a sauce that is equal parts soy sauce and sugar and then served over rice. Simplicity at its finest!

Yields 6 servings

⅛ cup soy sauce

⅛ cup granulated sugar

8 boneless, skinless chicken thighs, cut into bite-sized pieces

1 tablespoon all-purpose flour

1 teaspoon kosher salt

½ teaspoon ground pepper

2 tablespoons extra virgin olive oil

1½ cups white rice, cooked according to package directions

¼ cup chopped green onions

2 tablespoons sesame seeds

In a small bowl, combine soy sauce and sugar and whisk to combine. Set aside.

In a large bowl, combine chicken thighs, flour, salt and pepper. Toss chicken until all pieces are coated in flour. In a large skillet over medium-high heat, add olive oil. Once oil is heated, add chicken. Saute until chicken is cooked through, about 5 minutes. Give the soy sauce mixture a final whisk and then pour over the chicken. Simmer, stirring often, until sugar is dissolved and mixture is slightly thickened, about 5 minutes.

Spread cooked rice onto a large serving platter. Pour chicken and sauce over the rice and sprinkle green onions and sesame seeds on top.

Slow-Cooker Tomato Basil Chicken

For the sake of familiarity, let's call this bruschetta chicken. Tomatoes and garlic made into a simple, chunky sauce, juicy chicken and fresh basil sprinkled all over it. It's light, fresh and made in a slow cooker. It isn't everyday you find a slow cooker recipe that isn't heavy and rich.

Yields 6 servings

6 boneless, skinless chicken breasts

Kosher salt and ground pepper, for seasoning

2 tablespoons extra virgin olive oil

10 Roma tomatoes, chopped

1 tablespoon balsamic vinegar

5 garlic cloves, minced

1 teaspoon kosher salt

¼ cup minced fresh basil

Shredded Parmesan cheese, for serving

Season chicken breasts on both sides with salt and pepper and set aside. In a large skillet over medium-high heat, add olive oil. Once the oil is heated, add 3 chicken breasts. Sear each chicken breast on both sides, about 5 minutes, until lightly browned, but not cooked through. Set aside and repeat with the three remaining chicken breasts.

Spray the pot of a slow cooker with non-stick spray. In the pot, combine tomatoes, vinegar and garlic. Mix well to combine. Set heat to high and add chicken breasts on top. Cook for 5 hours. Remove chicken breasts and set aside on a plate. With a slotted spoon, transfer tomato chunks to a serving platter, discarding any extra liquid. Sprinkle salt over the tomatoes. Set chicken breasts on top. Sprinkle with basil and Parmesan cheese.

Sesame Udon Noodles with Chicken & Broccoli

Ever cooked udon noodles? They aren't prepared like regular noodles or pasta. It's not as simple as filling a pot with water and boiling. Udon noodles require a bit more attention. But the package will have directions, so no worries. It's simple enough. These udon noodles get all dressed up with a few veggies, chicken and a super flavorful dressing brimming with ginger, sesame oil and garlic. My three children and husband eat this like it's their last meal.

Yields 6 servings

For the noodles:

1 boneless, skinless chicken breast

Extra virgin olive oil, for seasoning

Kosher salt and ground pepper, for seasoning

1 12-ounce package uncooked udon noodles, prepared according to package directions

1 cup bite-sized broccoli florets

½ red bell pepper, diced

¼ cup chopped green onions

2 tablespoons sesame seeds

For the dressing:

⅛ cup soy sauce

¼ cup vegetable oil

3 tablespoons rice vinegar

3 tablespoons sesame oil

1 tablespoon freshly grated ginger

1 tablespoon honey

2 garlic cloves, minced

Preheat oven to 400 degrees F. Set chicken breast on a baking sheet. Rub on a small amount of olive oil and season with salt and pepper. Roast for 25-30 minutes, or until an inserted thermometer reaches 165 degrees F. Allow to cool, chop into bite-sized pieces and set aside.

While the chicken cooks, make the dressing. In a medium bowl, combine soy sauce, vegetable oil, rice vinegar, sesame oil, ginger, honey and garlic. Whisk until well combined and set aside.

In a large bowl, combine cooked udon noodles, broccoli, red bell pepper, green onions and sesame seeds. Pour dressing over the top and toss well to combine.

Serve immediately or refrigerate and serve chilled. Do not refrigerate overnight, because the noodles will get mushy.

Honey Almond-Glazed Chicken

When I was in the hospital after having my third baby, I was brought the evening's meal from the hospital cafeteria. With low expectations, I took off the plate cover and it revealed a surprisingly impressive meal. Steamed fresh green beans, perfectly seasoned. A light, fluffy Parker House roll with soft butter. And then a juicy chicken breast covered in the most heavenly honey glaze and sprinkled with almonds. Either I was starving or this was a standout hospital meal, if those even exist. I took great note of the chicken's flavor and put a reminder in the back of my mind to replicate it. Years later, I have figured it out. This chicken is not only simple in flavor, but also simple in preparation. I would say no more than 30 minutes until you and yours are around the table enjoying my favorite hospital dinner.

Yields 6 servings

½ cup all-purpose flour

1 teaspoon kosher salt

½ teaspoon ground pepper

¼ cup sliced almonds

2 tablespoons extra virgin olive oil

3 chicken breasts, halved horizontally

½ cup honey

1 teaspoon white wine vinegar

In a shallow dish, combine flour, salt and pepper. Whisk until combined. Dredge chicken breast halves in the flour mixture until both sides are coated. Shake off the excess. Repeat with remaining chicken breasts and set aside.

In a large skillet over medium heat, add almonds. Toast almonds until they are fragrant and lightly browned, about 8-10 minutes. Pour almonds into a small bowl and set aside.

In the same skillet, add olive oil. Once the oil is heated, add three chicken breast halves and brown on both sides until chicken is cooked through, about 10-15 minutes, or until an inserted thermometer reaches 165 degrees F. Set chicken on a serving platter and set aside. Repeat with remaining chicken breasts.

Once all the chicken breasts are cooked, make the glaze. Discard any remaining oil and flour. Once cleaned out, put the pan back on the heat and pour in the honey and vinegar. Simmer for 2 minutes. Pour honey glaze directly over the chicken breasts on the platter. Sprinkle toasted almonds over the top. Serve immediately.

Braised Chicken with Mushrooms & Red Onions

This dish was born out of the need to empty my fridge of ingredients about to turn. Mushrooms, rosemary and half a red onion. In all honesty, I probably should have tossed the mushrooms, but once cooked, no one knew. Once I got the chicken simmering and my house smelling divine, you would never have know those ingredients were headed for the trash the next day. The chicken was incredibly tender, no need for a knife. The mushrooms and onions flavored the sauce so perfectly, and all that garlic helped too. Rice came in to soak up the sauce, and we had ourselves a dinner that never seemed like vegetables about to go bad.

Yields 6 servings.

2 tablespoons extra virgin olive oil

6 boneless, skinless chicken thighs

2 tablespoons unsalted butter

1 pound white mushrooms, thinly sliced

½ red onion, thinly sliced

4 garlic cloves, minced

1 tablespoon fresh rosemary, minced

1 teaspoon kosher salt

½ teaspoon ground pepper

2 tablespoons all-purpose flour

2 cups low-sodium chicken stock

1½ cups white rice, cooked according to package directions

In a large skillet over medium-high heat, add olive oil. Once the oil is heated, add 3 chicken thighs. Sear chicken on both sides until lightly browned, but not cooked all the way through. Remove chicken from the pan and set aside. Repeat with the remaining 3 chicken thighs.

Once chicken is seared and set aside, add butter, mushrooms, red onion, garlic, rosemary, salt and pepper to the skillet. Saute, stirring occasionally, until mushrooms and onions are softened, about 10 minutes. Add flour and saute until flour is lightly browned and there is no flour smell, about 5 minutes. Pour in chicken stock, stir well and set chicken thighs on top of the mushrooms and onions. Reduce heat to low, cover and simmer for 25-30 minutes, or until an inserted thermometer reaches 165 degrees F.

Serve braised chicken and vegetables with a spoonful of sauce over rice.

Curry and Yogurt Roast Chicken

When my first son was just a baby, we would go on our little dates to the farmer's market in the center of town in Glendora, CA. As I pushed his stroller along, we would see giant strawberries, bright peonies and cover bands playing top 80's hits. And my favorite, the man selling Indian food from his small food cart. We would stand in the long line, smelling the curry and naan, and wait impatiently for a kebab and hummus. With our styrofoam box and plastic forks, we would find a shady bench and feast. Hot, tender spiced chicken dipped in cold garlic hummus was a bit of nirvana. This chicken takes me back there every time. The chicken is simply marinated in yogurt and spices and then roasted. It's as juicy as can be and slathered in flavor. Just get some naan and hummus and you are set.

Yields 6 servings

2 cups plain yogurt

3 teaspoons curry powder

1 teaspoon garam masala

1 teaspoon ground coriander

1 teaspoon turmeric

8 bone-in chicken legs, thighs or both

Kosher salt, for seasoning

In a medium bowl, combine yogurt, curry powder, garam masala, coriander and turmeric. Whisk until well combined. Add chicken to a zip top bag and pour yogurt mixture over the top. Seal the bag tightly and press the yogurt mixture around the chicken. Let marinate in the fridge for at least 1 hour or up to 6 hours.

Preheat oven to 450 degrees F. Spray a broiler pan with non-stick spray. Or alternately, use a cooling rack set into a baking sheet. Set chicken on top and season lightly with salt. Roast for 45-50 minutes, or until an inserted thermometer reaches 165 degrees F.

Sesame Ginger Turkey Sliders

This is a nice way to change and lighten up a burger. First, ground turkey is always a great low-calorie, high-protein option. Then ginger and sesame oil add a little variety from the traditional mustard-and-ketchup hamburger. These could work as dinner, with each family member getting two sliders or you could do these as appetizers.

Yields 6 servings

2 pounds ground turkey breast

1 garlic clove, minced

1½ teaspoons kosher salt

¾ teaspoon toasted sesame oil

½ teaspoon grated fresh ginger

½ teaspoon ground pepper

1 egg, beaten

6 tablespoons extra virgin olive oil, divided

12 dinner rolls, sliced in half lengthwise

1 8-ounce can crushed pineapple, drained

Mayonnaise, for serving

2 Roma tomatoes, thinly sliced

A few green leaf lettuce leaves

In a large bowl, add ground turkey, garlic, salt, sesame oil, ginger, pepper and beaten egg. Combine all ingredients, but do not over-mix. Separate ground turkey mixture into quarters. Separate each quarter into thirds. Shape each third into ¼ inch thick patties.

In a large skillet over medium-high heat, add 2 tablespoons olive oil. Once the oil is heated, add 4 ground turkey patties and cook on each side for 5 minutes, or until an inserted thermometer reaches 165 degrees F. Repeat with the remaining olive oil and ground turkey patties.

To serve, spread a small spoonful of crushed pineapple onto the bottom half of the roll. Spread mayo on the top half. Place one ground turkey patty on top of the pineapple, add a tomato and torn lettuce leaf. Add the top bun and serve.

Beef

Grilled Hamburgers 36

Pan-Seared London Broil Steak with Carmelized Onions 39

Meatloaf & Mushroom Brown Gravy 40

Slow-Cooker Roast Beef with Root Vegetables & Gravy 43

Cornbread & Beef Bake with Sweet Potatoes 44
& Green Chiles

Ethan's Orange & Herb Marinated Tri-tip Steak 47

Grilled Ribeye Steaks with Rosemary Gorgonzola Butter 48

Korean Beef Lettuce Wraps with Spicy Mayo 51

Meatball & Mozzarella Sub Sandwiches 52

Braised Herb & Cheese Stuffed Flank Steak 55

Grilled Hamburgers

Grilled burgers and summer go together like Lucy and Ethel, but don't feel bad if you have a craving and find yourself standing in the snow, grilling. Grilled burgers are my husband's specialty. Stick these on a soft bun and add whatever toppings you and yours prefer. My perfect burger is mustard, ketchup, avocado, green leaf lettuce, red onion, a bit of dill pickle and a perfect, juicy tomato slice.

Yields 6 servings

1½ pounds ground beef, preferably 80% lean 20% fat

Kosher salt and ground pepper, for seasoning

Worcestershire sauce, for seasoning

6 thin slices of cheddar cheese, if making cheeseburgers

6 hamburger buns, for serving

Separate ground beef into six even portions. Shape each portion into 5 inch patties. Season each patty with salt and pepper on each side.

Set grill to high. Once heated, grill burgers for 5 minutes, flipping over half way through. Once finished, drizzle a small amount of worcestershire sauce on top. If adding cheese for cheeseburgers, season with the worcestershire sauce and then add cheese during the last minute of grilling.

After grilling, assemble burgers with your preferred toppings.

Pan-Seared London Broil Steak with Caramelized Onions

Years ago, I worked as the receptionist at a car dealership in Southern California. We had a guy come in every so often selling prepared meals during lunchtime. One of the meals was a London broil steak, and still to this day, it is the best London broil I have ever had. It was so tender, almost like a filet and the steak was so rich in flavor. Here is my best effort at recreating that dish. I added caramelized onions just because I love 'em. Not sure what cut a London broil is? It's usually a top round steak. A lot of butchers label it "London broil," but if you can't find that, a flank steak will do the job just fine.

Yields 6 servings

2 tablespoons extra virgin olive oil

3 yellow onions, halved and thinly sliced

1½ teaspoons kosher salt

1 teaspoon worcestershire sauce

½ teaspoon ground pepper

1 London broil steak, about 2-2½ lbs.

Kosher salt and ground pepper, for seasoning

In a large oven-safe skillet over medium heat, add olive oil, onions, kosher salt, Worcestershire sauce and ground pepper. Stir well to combine, cover and allow onions to caramelize, stirring occasionally, for 1 hour.

While the onions caramelize, season the steak with salt and pepper on both sides. Once onions are caramelized, transfer to a small bowl. Preheat the oven to 350 degrees F. Set the pan back on the heat, set to medium-high and add steak. Sear the steak on both sides until golden brown, about 2 minutes on each side. Set the pan into the oven and roast until the steak's internal temperature is 130 degrees F for medium rare, about 5 minutes.

Set the steak onto a cutting board, loosely cover with foil and let rest for 10 minutes. Slice steak against the grain and set onto a serving platter. Garnish with the caramelized onions.

Meatloaf with Mushroom Brown Gravy

This one is for my husband, who has always claimed to hate meatloaf. Well, not anymore. I took on the challenge to make a great meatloaf with a mouth-watering gravy to sop up. And I did it! This isn't the meatloaf that gets a bad reputation. This one is moist, full of flavor and has a delicious mushroom gravy on top. It's a great way to give meatloaf the respect it deserves.

Yields 6 servings

For the meatloaf:

2 tablespoons extra virgin olive oil

½ yellow onion, diced

1 teaspoon kosher salt

½ teaspoon ground pepper

2 garlic cloves, minced

1 teaspoon worcestershire sauce

1 pound ground beef

1 pound ground pork

1 cup bread crumbs

1 egg, beaten

½ cup tomato sauce

For the gravy:

1 tablespoon extra virgin olive oil

½ yellow onion, diced

1 garlic clove, minced

1 8-ounce package sliced mushrooms

½ teaspoon kosher salt

¼ teaspoon ground pepper

2 cups beef stock

½ teaspoon worcestershire sauce

2 tablespoons butter, softened

2 tablespoons all-purpose flour

Preheat oven to 350 degrees F.

For the meatloaf, in a large skillet over medium heat, add olive oil. Once the oil is heated, add diced onion, salt and pepper. Saute until onions are softened, about 10 minutes. Add the garlic and worcestershire sauce and saute for 1 minute. Once sauteed, transfer onions and garlic to a small bowl and set aside to cool.

In a large bowl, add beef, pork, bread crumbs, egg, tomato sauce, cooled onions and garlic. Gently mix until combined, but do not over mix. Add meat mixture to a 9x13 inch pan and shape it into a loaf. Bake meatloaf for 60-70 minutes, or until an inserted thermometer reaches 160 degrees F.

While the meatloaf bakes, make the gravy. Set the large skillet used to saute the onion over medium-high heat. Add olive oil. Once the oil is heated, add the onions, garlic, mushrooms, salt and pepper. Saute until onions and mushrooms are softened, about 5 minutes. Pour in the beef stock and worcestershire, bring to a simmer. Combine softened butter and flour in a small bowl and mix into a paste. Reduce heat to medium and with a whisk, add butter and flour paste to beef stock mixture and stir in until butter is melted. Continue to simmer and stir occasionally until the gravy is thickened, about 5 minutes.

Slice meatloaf and serve with gravy over the top.

Meatloaf with Mushroom Brown Gravy
Walnut Green Beans, Pg. 179

Slow-Cooker Roast Beef with Root Vegetables & Gravy

Growing up, roast beef was synonymous with the word Sunday. I remember my mom getting up early to head over to the church to attend to her church duties and, before she would leave, she would start our Sunday roast. Then a few hours later, when we would all come home from church and pull the car into the garage, we could smell the roast. Robust, rich beef, tender as can be and paired with a drizzle of gravy. As a bonus, root vegetables are cooked with the roast, so this is a one-pot meal.

Yields 6 servings.

2 tablespoons minced fresh rosemary, divided

2 tablespoons minced fresh sage, divided

3 teaspoons kosher salt, divided

1½ teaspoons ground pepper, divided

3-3½ pounds boneless beef chuck roast

2 onions, halved and quartered

3 russet potatoes, chopped

3 carrots, peeled and sliced

2 cups beef stock

1 teaspoon Worcestershire sauce

1 garlic clove, minced

1/2 teaspoon kosher salt

½ teaspoon garlic powder

½ teaspoon onion powder

4 tablespoons butter, softened

4 tablespoons all purpose flour

In a small bowl, combine 1 tablespoon rosemary, 1 tablespoon sage, 1½ teaspoons salt and 1 teaspoon pepper. Mix well. Rub seasoning mixture on the beef roast, pressing so the seasoning adheres. Set beef roast aside.

In a large slow-cooker, add onions in an even layer on the bottom. Add potatoes and carrots on top. Sprinkle remaining rosemary, sage, salt and pepper on top. In a small bowl, whisk together the beef stock, Worcestershire sauce and garlic. Pour over the vegetables. Set the beef roast on top of the vegetables. Set heat to high and cook for 6 hours.

Once the roast is cooked, or an inserted thermometer reaches 160 degrees F, set meat on a cutting board to rest and cover loosely with foil. With a slotted spoon, remove onions, potatoes and carrots to a serving platter. Pour remaining liquid in the slow cooker through a strainer and into a large skillet over medium heat. Stir in ½ teaspoon salt, garlic powder and onion powder. Once the liquid is simmering, combine the softened butter and flour in a small bowl and stir well, making a paste. Whisk the paste into the simmering liquid. Stir until butter is melted and liquid is thickened. Taste and season with additional salt if needed. Simmer the gravy for 5 minutes.

Slice the roast beef and serve roast beef and vegetables with gravy on top.

Cornbread & Beef Bake with Sweet Potatoes & Green Chiles

Your sister came to town with her loud, sticky, wonderful children. While your children are in heaven playing with their cousins and being up to no good, you are having a hard time keeping those bottomless stomachs full. Between Transformer tyranny and Barbie soirees, the PB & J's just aren't cutting it. Try out this dish. A whole meal in a pan. Meaty ground beef made more substantial with sweet potatoes and green chiles, and with cornbread batter baked on top. Not fans of sweet potatoes and green chiles? Too bad for you. But you can just do your family's favorite potato and omit the green chiles altogether.

Yields 8 servings

For the ground beef:

2 tablespoons extra virgin olive oil
1 yellow onion, diced
1 sweet potato, peeled and small diced
2 teaspoons kosher salt
½ teaspoon ground pepper
3 garlic cloves, minced
2 pounds ground beef
1 4-ounce can diced green chiles
1 15-ounce can diced tomatoes
1/2 cup water
¼ cup tomato paste

For the cornbread:

1½ cups cornmeal
1 cup all-purpose flour
1½ teaspoons baking powder
1 teaspoon salt
½ cup sugar
1¼ cups milk
2 eggs
¼ cup vegetable oil

Preheat oven to 375 degrees F.

For the ground beef, set a large skillet over medium heat, add olive oil. Once the oil is heated, add the onions, sweet potato, salt and pepper. Saute until the onions are softened, about 10 minutes. Add the garlic and saute for 1 additional minute.

Turn the heat up to medium-high and add the ground beef. Saute and break up the meat with a wooden spoon. Once cooked through, add the green chiles, tomatoes, water and tomato paste. Stir well and cook for an additional 5 minutes. Pour mixture into a 9x13 inch pan. With the wooden spoon, spread the mixture evenly through the pan. Set aside.

For the cornbread, in a large bowl, combine cornmeal, flour, baking powder, salt and sugar. Whisk well to combine and set aside. In a small bowl, combine milk, eggs and vegetable oil and whisk. Pour milk mixture into the cornmeal mixture and stir well, leaving no lumps. Pour cornbread batter over the ground beef mixture.

Bake for 35-40 minutes, until the cornbread is golden brown and an inserted toothpick comes out clean.

Ethan's Orange & Herb Marinated Tri-tip Steak

Recipe by Ethan Ingram

If you aren't familiar with tri-tip, you should take some time to get to know it. The tri-tip cut of beef is from the bottom sirloin of a cow. It is a small, triangular muscle that is tender and flavorful as can be. My husband uses tri-tip frequently for catered events, this recipe in particular. A sweet, savory marinade covers the meat, preferably overnight, then it is grilled and finished in the oven. The result is a juicy, flavor-packed steak that you will have a hard time saving for leftovers.

Yields 6 servings

½ cup extra virgin olive oil

⅓ cup orange marmalade

⅓ cup soy sauce

¼ cup honey

¼ cup red wine vinegar

2 tablespoons minced fresh rosemary

1 teaspoon kosher salt

1 teaspoon ground pepper

3 garlic cloves, minced

1 tri-tip roast, about 2-2½ pounds

In a large bowl, combine olive oil, marmalade, soy sauce, honey, red wine vinegar, rosemary, salt, pepper and garlic. Whisk well and add tri-tip, submerging as much of the meat as possible. Cover and refrigerate for at least 6 hours or up to 24 hours.

Preheat oven to 400 degrees F and set grill to high. Once grill is hot, remove tri-tip from the marinade and grill, discarding the marinade. Grill, uncovered for 5 minutes, flipping halfway through, just until each side has grill marks. Transfer meat to a baking sheet and put in the oven. Roast until the internal temperature reaches 130 degrees F for medium rare, about 10 minutes.

Set tri-tip onto a cutting board, loosely cover with foil and let rest for 10-15 minutes. Cut tri-tip in half crosswise and then slice each half lengthwise, against the grain.

Grilled Ribeye Steaks with Rosemary Gorgonzola Butter

When I was growing up, the New Year's Eve tradition in my family was grilled steak. Even if it was snowing--grilled steak. I remember seeing my dad out on the patio in a coat, hat, gloves and boots, grilling our New Year's Eve tradition. As we would ring in the new year, we would devour juicy, tender ribeyes. Unlike my family's, this steak isn't alone. It has a savory grill butter. Right as the steak comes off the grill, add a bit of the grill butter on top and let the gorgonzola melt into the meat and the herbs flavor the steak. Leftover butter? I am certain it would be delicious mixed into mashed potatoes.

Yields 6 servings.

¼ cup unsalted butter, softened

1 garlic clove, minced

2 tablespoons chopped gorgonzola cheese

1 tablespoon fresh rosemary, minced

1 teaspoon Worcestershire sauce

6 ribeye steaks, with or without bone

Kosher salt and ground pepper for seasoning

In a medium bowl, combine butter, garlic, gorgonzola cheese, rosemary and Worcestershire sauce. With a rubber scraper, mix until well combined. Set aside.

Heat grill to high. Season each steak with salt and pepper. Once grill is hot, add steaks. Grill, uncovered, on the first side for 5 minutes. Flip and grill for an additional 3 minutes. Set steaks aside on a platter. Add a spoonful of rosemary gorgonzola butter onto each steak. Allow steaks to rest for 5 minutes before serving.

Grilled Ribeye Steaks with
Rosemary Gorgonzola Butter

Bulgur Pilaf with Red Peppers
& Almonds, Pg. 186

Korean Beef Lettuce Wraps with Spicy Mayo

*When your neighbor calls and asks, "Do you want to come over for sushi making lessons?"
you head right over. My neighbor, Heidi, made a Korean-style sushi roll full of bulgogi, a Korean
beef that is sweet and salty. It stuck with me and I knew I was going to have to do something
with it. So here is bulgogi-flavored ground beef in a crisp romaine leaf with some rice, crunchy
veggies and a creamy, spicy mayo on top. Not feeling the lettuce part of this? Just make a rice
bowl with the beef and veggies on top. That is what I usually do for my kids.*

Yields 6 servings

For the mayo:

½ cup mayonnaise

2 garlic cloves, minced

1 teaspoon Sriracha chile sauce

1 teaspoon toasted sesame oil

For the ground beef:

⅔ cup soy sauce

2 tablespoons cornstarch

⅔ cup brown sugar

2 teaspoons toasted sesame oil

1 teaspoon rice vinegar

1½ pounds ground beef

3 garlic cloves, minced

1½ teaspoons kosher salt

1 head romaine lettuce, leaves torn off the core

1 cup long grain white rice, cooked according to package directions

1 bunch green onions, chopped

1 cup mung bean sprouts

2 cups shredded carrots

In a small bowl, add mayonnaise, garlic, Sriracha and sesame oil. Whisk well to combine and set aside.

Measure soy sauce into a liquid measuring cup. Once measured, reserve 2 tablespoons in a small bowl. Add the cornstarch to the reserved soy sauce and mix well. Set aside. In a medium bowl, add remaining soy sauce, brown sugar, sesame oil and rice vinegar. Whisk well to combine and set aside.

In a large skillet over medium-high heat, add ground beef, garlic and salt. Saute until ground beef is cooked through, about 10 minutes. Pour in brown sugar mixture. Stir well. Once simmering, stir in cornstarch mixture. Stir well and simmer until thickened. Remove pan from the heat.

To assemble, line a romaine leaf with cooked rice and add a big spoonful of ground beef. Sprinkle on green onions, sprouts and carrots and then drizzle spicy mayo on top.

Meatball & Mozzarella Sub Sandwiches

My cute kids call these "pizza sandwiches." I remember the first time I set these in front of them for dinner. My 4 year old squealed with glee and said, "Mom! You put pizza into a sandwich!" Of course I went along with it and said, "Yes! Just for you!" Hey, whatever gets my kids eating their dinner. These sandwiches can please the kids as much as the adults. The delicious meatballs and savory sauce with melty mozzarella on top are super satisfying for everyone.

Yields 6 servings

For the meatballs:
1½ pounds ground beef
1 cup panko bread crumbs
⅓ cup shredded Parmesan cheese
1½ teaspoons kosher salt
1 teaspoon ground pepper
1 teaspoon Worcestershire sauce
1 teaspoon garlic powder

For the sandwiches:
6 hoagie rolls, split lengthwise
1½ cups shredded mozzarella cheese

For the sauce:
2 tablespoons extra virgin olive oil
½ yellow onion, diced
½ green bell pepper, diced
1 teaspoon kosher salt
½ teaspoon ground pepper
3 garlic cloves, minced
2 teaspoons tomato paste
1 15-ounce can diced tomatoes
1 15-ounce can tomato sauce
1 teaspoon dried basil

Preheat oven to 350 degrees F. Spray a baking sheet with non-stick spray.

In a large bowl, combine ground beef, bread crumbs, Parmesan cheese, salt, pepper, Worcestershire sauce and garlic powder. Mix well, but be sure not to over mix. Split the ground beef mixture in half and then split each half into half again. You should have four small piles of ground beef mixture. Portion each pile into 6 rolled meatballs, making 24 meatballs total. Set meatballs onto the prepared baking sheet and bake for 15-20 minutes, or until an inserted thermometer reaches 160 degrees F.

While the meatballs bake, make the sauce. In a large skillet over medium heat, add olive oil. Once the oil is heated, add onion, green bell pepper, salt and pepper. Saute until vegetables are softened, about 10 minutes. Add garlic and tomato paste and saute until the paste is broken up and the onions take on the red color. Pour in the diced tomatoes and tomato sauce. Stir in basil. Simmer for 10 minutes. Once the meatballs are finished baking, add them to the sauce and stir well, coating the meatballs in sauce.

Heat broiler to low. Pull out a small amount of bread from the bottom half of the hoagie rolls, making a well for the meatballs. Set both top and bottom roll halves onto a baking sheet.

Fill each well with 4 meatballs and some sauce spooned on top. Sprinkle mozzarella cheese on top of the meatballs and put under the broiler. Broil until cheese is melted and bread is toasted, about 3 minutes. Remove top rolls from under the broiler if they begin to brown too quickly. Top each sandwich with the other half of the roll.

Braised Herb and Cheese Stuffed Flank Steak

This is a great dish for a Sunday dinner, Christmas dinner or any special occasion during colder weather when your oven will warm up your house. Flank steak is rolled up with two kinds of cheese and fresh herbs then braised in marinara sauce. The result is a rich and tender steak, with a sauce that has mixed with all of the rich beef flavors. It's the perfect way to help dress up any formal meal.

Yields 6 servings

For the steak:

½ cup panko bread crumbs

½ cup shredded Parmesan

½ cup shredded Romano cheese

2 tablespoons fresh flat-leaf parsley, Minced

2 tablespoons fresh rosemary, minced

1 flank steak, about 1-1½ pounds

Kitchen twine, for tying up the steak

Kosher salt and ground pepper, for seasoning

2 tablespoons extra virgin olive oil

For the sauce:

2 tablespoons extra virgin olive oil

1 yellow onion, diced

1 teaspoon kosher salt

½ teaspoon ground pepper

2 garlic cloves, minced

1 tablespoon tomato paste

1 15-ounce can diced tomatoes

2 15-ounce can tomato sauce

2 teaspoons dried Italian seasoning blend

Preheat oven to 350 degrees F.

In a medium bowl, combine panko bread crumbs, parmesan, romano, parsley and rosemary. Mix well to combine and set aside. Lay the flank steak out on a work surface. Evenly spread all of bread crumb mixture over the flank steak. Starting with the short end, tightly roll up the steak to the other short end. Tie tightly with the kitchen twine. Season all sides of the rolled steak with salt and pepper.

In a large oven-proof pot over medium high heat, add olive oil. Once the oil is heated, sear the rolled steak on all sides, but not cooking all the way through. Set rolled steak onto a plate and set aside.

Now make the sauce. Set the pot back on the heat and reduce heat to medium. Add the olive oil. Once the oil is heated, add onion, salt and pepper. Saute until the onion is softened, about 10 minutes. Add garlic and tomato paste and saute until the paste is broken up and the onions take on the red color. Pour in the diced tomatoes, tomato sauce and Italian seasoning. Simmer for 10 minutes, stirring occasionally. Set rolled flank steak on the sauce. Cover the pot, set it in the oven and braise for 1½ hours, until sauce is thickened and steak is cooked through or an inserted thermometer reaches at least 135 degrees F. Set stuffed flank steak onto a cutting board. Cut off kitchen twine and slice into 6 slices. Serve with a spoonful of marinara sauce.

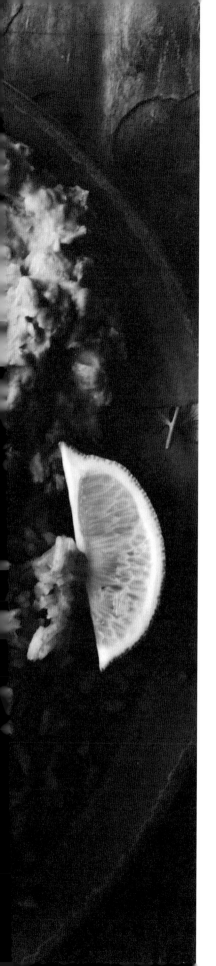

Pork

Ham and Cheese Frittata 59

Slow-Cooker Herbed Pork Loin Roast with Gravy 60

Pan-Seared Pork Chops with Apricot Sage Sauce 63

Roasted Pork Tenderloin with Pomegranate Honey Sauce 64

Ethan's Grilled Baby-Back Ribs with Whitney's 67
Homemade Barbecue Sauce

Pulled Pork Sandwiches with Coleslaw 68

Baked Sweet and Sour Pork Chops 71

Shredded Sweet Pork Tacos 72

Ham & Cheese Frittata
Potato Pancakes, Pg. 185

Ham & Cheese Frittata

Such a quicky dish that goes for breakfast, lunch or dinner. I keep diced ham in ½ cup portions in the freezer just for this frittata. Maybe some of you are asking: "What is a frittata?" It can be explained as an egg pizza. Eggs whisked and poured over sauteed ham. A bit of cheese is added and then it is put into the oven to set. Besides being easy, it's also inexpensive.

Yields 6 servings

8 eggs

2 tablespoons water

½ teaspoon kosher salt

¼ teaspoon ground pepper

1 teaspoon unsalted butter

½ cup diced ham

½ cup shredded cheddar cheese

¼ cup sliced green onions, for serving

Preheat oven to 400 degrees F.

In a medium bowl, combine eggs, water, salt and pepper. Whisk well, until eggs are broken up and smooth. Set aside.

In a small non-stick skillet over medium-high heat, add butter. Once butter is melted, add ham. Saute until ham is lightly browned, about 2 minutes. Pour in eggs and add ¼ cup cheddar cheese. Gently mix the cheese in and then allow the egg to set on the edges. Once the egg has begun to set, sprinkle remaining cheese on top and then put the pan in the oven. Bake for 10-12 minutes, or until frittata is set in the middle.

With a rubber scraper, loosen the edges of the frittata and transfer it to a cutting board. Slice into wedges and serve. Garnish with green onions.

Slow-Cooker Herbed Pork Loin Roast with Gravy

The slow-cooker does it again. This roast is easy, with few ingredients, juicy results and plenty for leftovers. No fresh herbs? Do dried. They will work just fine. And whatever you do, make sure you serve this with a big pile of mashed potatoes. Who ever heard of gravy without mashed potatoes?

Yields 6 servings

1 tablespoon fresh rosemary, minced

1 tablespoon fresh sage, minced

3 teaspoons kosher salt

2 teaspoons ground pepper

2½-3 pounds pork loin roast

2 tablespoons extra virgin olive oil

1½ cups low-sodium chicken stock

½ teaspoon garlic powder

¼ cup unsalted butter, softened

¼ cup all-purpose flour

Kosher salt, for seasoning

In a small bowl, combine rosemary, sage, salt and pepper. Mix well. Rub seasoning mixture on the pork roast, pressing so the seasoning adheres. Set aside.

In a large skillet over medium-high heat, add olive oil. Once the oil is heated, add the pork roast. Sear the pork roast on all sides, but not cooking all the way through. Set seared pork roast into a large slow-cooker. Pour in chicken stock. Set heat to high and cook for 5 hours.

Once the roast is cooked, set on a cutting board to rest and cover loosely with foil. Measure out 2 cups of the liquid in the bottom of the slow-cooker. Pour the liquid through a wire mesh strainer into the large skillet, discarding the fat and herbs in the strainer. Stir in garlic powder. Set heat to medium and bring liquid to a simmer. Once the liquid is simmering, combine the softened butter and flour in a small bowl and stir well, making a paste. Whisk the paste into the simmering liquid. Stir until the butter is melted and the liquid is thickened. Taste and season with additional salt if needed. Simmer the gravy for 5 minutes.

Slice the pork roast and serve with gravy on top.

Pan-Seared Pork Chops
with Apricot Sage Sauce

Braised Kale, Pg. 169

Pan-Seared Pork Chops with Apricot Sage Sauce

Pork and apricot, two of the best pals around. Pork is naturally sweet, so any fruit companion is welcome to the party. This apricot sage sauce is the perfect balance of sweet and savory. Onions, garlic and sage combine with apricot jam for a sweet, sticky sauce over juicy, seared pork chops. Too hot inside the kitchen to cook? Cook these pork chops on your grill and make the sauce in a saucepan on the grill as well.

Yields 6 servings

6 thin cut, bone-in pork chops

Kosher salt and ground pepper

6 tablespoons extra virgin olive oil, divided

½ red onion, thinly sliced

½ teaspoon kosher salt

½ teaspoon ground pepper

2 garlic cloves, minced

1 tablespoon minced fresh sage

1 cup low-sodium chicken stock

½ cup apricot jam

Season both sides of the pork chops with salt and pepper and set aside.

In a large skillet over medium-high heat, add 2 tablespoons of olive oil. Once the oil is heated, add three of the pork chops. Sear on both sides for about 5 minutes, until the pork chops are cooked through, or until an inserted thermometer reaches 160 degrees F. Remove pork chops from the pan onto a plate and cover with foil to keep warm. Repeat with the remaining pork chops and two tablespoons of olive oil.

Turn the heat down to medium. Add remaining 2 tablespoons of olive oil. Once the oil is heated, add the onion, salt and pepper. Saute onion until softened, about 5 minutes. Add garlic and sage and saute for 1 additional minute. Add chicken broth and simmer until reduced by half, about 5 minutes. Stir in apricot jam. Simmer for 3 minutes. Pour into a small bowl and serve over finished pork chops.

Roasted Pork Tenderloin with Pomegranate Honey Sauce

What a dramatic dish! Dark red pomegranate honey sauce drizzled over beautiful roasted pork tenderloin. Naturally sweet pork and tart pomegranate sauce marry perfectly. A word to the wise, watch that sauce carefully as it begins to thicken. It takes some time to get to the point where it will thicken, but once it does, quick as a wink, that sauce will burn. So watch it carefully!

Yields 6 servings

2 16-ounce bottles pomegranate juice

¼ cup honey

2 teaspoons dijon mustard

2-2½ pounds pork tenderloin, about 2 separate tenderloins

Kosher salt and ground pepper, for seasoning

2 tablespoons extra virgin olive oil

In a medium skillet over medium-high heat, pour in both bottles of pomegranate juice. Let simmer, stirring occasionally, until significantly reduced and thickened, about 35-40 minutes. Once pomegranate juice is reduced and coats the back of a wooden spoon, pour into a small bowl. It should yield about ½ cup. Stir in honey and dijon mustard. Set aside to cool.

Preheat oven to 400 degrees F. Spray a baking sheet with non-stick spray and set aside.

Season each tenderloin with salt and pepper.

In a large skillet over high heat, add olive oil. Once the oil is heated, add both tenderloins and brown on all sides, but not cooking the tenderloins all the way through. Transfer tenderloins to the prepared baking sheet and roast for 20-25 minutes, or until the internal temperature reaches 165 F. Once roasted, cover loosely with foil and let rest for 15 minutes.

Slice pork tenderloin into 1-inch thick slices. Transfer to a serving platter and serve tenderloin with a small drizzle of pomegranate honey sauce.

Roasted Pork Tenderloin with Pomegranate Honey Sauce
Roasted Brussel Sprouts with Browned Butter, Pg. 176

Ethan's Grilled Baby-Back Ribs with
Whitney's Homemade Barbecue Sauce

Roasted Red Potatoes with Rosemary, Pg. 168

Ethan's Grilled Baby-Back Ribs with Whitney's Homemade Barbecue Sauce

My husband spent years perfecting the method of tender, flavorful ribs. People, the process had me eating all sorts of tough, unappetizing ribs, but somebody had to do it. These are a masterpiece. This recipe produces the cliche that is too often attached to baby-back ribs. But truly, these do "fall off the bone." What makes them so irresistible? The perfect sweet and tangy barbecue sauce. This recipe is most definitely worth the effort. I could see these being the perfect thing to make on Father's Day for the father figure in your life. You know, men and their apparent "thing" for grilled meat.

Yields 6 servings

For the ribs:

3 tablespoons kosher salt

3 tablespoons brown sugar

2 teaspoons ground pepper

2 teaspoons garlic powder

2 teaspoons onion powder

½ teaspoon cayenne powder

½ teaspoon paprika

2 racks pork baby-back ribs

For the barbecue sauce:

1½ cups ketchup

1 cup brown sugar

½ cup apple cider vinegar

2 tablespoons soy sauce

2 tablespoons Worcestershire sauce

1 tablespoon honey

1 tablespoon vegetable oil

1½ teaspoons molasses

½ teaspoon ground ginger

¼ teaspoon liquid smoke

2 garlic cloves, minced

Preheat oven to 400 degrees F.

In a small bowl, combine salt, brown sugar, pepper, garlic powder, onion powder, cayenne powder and paprika. Stir well to combine and set aside. Tear off two large sheets of foil and set one rib rack on each one. Sprinkle both sides of the racks evenly with the seasoning mix. Top each rack with another piece of foil and seal all around the edges. Set wrapped rib racks onto a large baking sheet. Bake in the oven for 2½ hours. Once baked, remove from oven and set aside.

While the ribs are baking, make the barbecue sauce. In a medium saucepan over medium heat, combine all barbecue sauce ingredients. Whisk well and simmer, stirring occasionally, for 30 minutes. Remove saucepan from heat and pour barbecue sauce into a small bowl and set aside.

Set grill to high. Once heated, unwrap rib racks and set on the grill. Grill on each side for 2 minutes, just to add grill marks. With a basting brush, generously brush each side with barbecue sauce generously. Grill on each side for an additional 3 minutes. Remove from the grill. Cut rib racks into individual ribs and set on a serving platter. Serve with remaining barbecue sauce for dipping.

Pulled Pork Sandwiches with Coleslaw

Barbecue sauce is the house sauce in my family. My children want it with everything. My 4-year-old even tried it on spaghetti. Eww! But hey, if it makes him clean his dinner plate, then so be it! This is my preferred method of barbecue sauce consumption. Rich, slow-cooked barbecue pork on a soft roll and topped with fresh, crisp coleslaw. The coleslaw is essential to having the complete experience. Leftovers? Make pizza! Pizza dough, spread on barbecue sauce then add shredded pork and mozzarella cheese. Bake and then add coleslaw on top. It's a whole new pizza experience.

Yields 8 servings.

For the sandwiches:

2 yellow onions, sliced

1 Boston butt pork roast, about 3-4 pounds, fat cap cut off

Kosher salt and ground pepper, for seasoning

6 whole cloves

¼ teaspoon liquid smoke

16-ounce bottle barbecue sauce

8 kaiser rolls, split

For the coleslaw:

16-ounce bag coleslaw mix

½ red onion, diced

1 green bell pepper, diced

2 tablespoons fresh flat-leaf parsley, minced

⅓ cup mayonnaise

3 tablespoons apple cider vinegar

1 teaspoon granulated sugar

½ teaspoon kosher salt

¼ teaspoon ground pepper

Place half of the sliced onions at the bottom of a slow cooker. Season the pork roast with salt and pepper and stud with whole cloves. Place roast in slow cooker on top of the sliced onion. Cover with the remaining sliced onion and add enough water to fill the slow cooker 2/3 of the way up. Add liquid smoke to the water. Cover and cook on low for 8 to 10 hours.

While the roast cooks, make the coleslaw. In a large bowl, add coleslaw mix, red onion, green bell pepper and parsley. In a small bowl, combine mayonnaise, vinegar, sugar, salt and pepper and whisk until well combined. Pour over coleslaw mixture and toss well. Cover and chill until serving time.

Remove roast and set onto a cutting board. Let sit until cool enough to handle. Remove the cloves from the roast and any remaining fat. Pour water and onions out of the slow cooker and discard. When the pork roast is cool enough to handle, use a fork or your fingers to pull it apart until the entire roast is shredded. Return the pulled pork to the slow cooker. Mix in the barbecue sauce and cover. Heat on high for 15 minutes. Mound a pile of pork on a kaiser roll and top with coleslaw.

Baked Sweet & Sour Pork Chops

Sweet and sour sauce reminds me of a tiny Chinese restaurant my parents used to take us to when my sisters and I were little girls. All six of us girls and my parents would pass around big plates of Chinese classics: garlic noodles, beef with broccoli, snow peas and sweet and sour chicken. The chicken was always my favorite. I loved taking extra sauce and mixing it with the noodles and the rice. Because of that, I would recommend you make up a pot of steamed rice to serve with this. Between bites of tasty pork, take a swipe of sauce and rice.

Yields 6 servings

6 boneless pork loin chops

Kosher salt and ground pepper, for seasoning

1 green bell pepper, thinly sliced

1 carrot, peeled and thinly sliced

1 20-ounce can pineapple chunks, drained and juices reserved

2 tablespoons cornstarch

½ cup granulated sugar

¼ cup apple cider vinegar

¼ cup ketchup

¼ cup soy sauce

½ teaspoon kosher salt

Preheat oven to 425 degrees F. Season each pork chop with salt and pepper and set into a 9x13 inch pan. Sprinkle green bell peppers, carrots and 1 cup pineapple chunks over the pork chops. Set aside.

In a small bowl, combine ⅓ cup pineapple juice and cornstarch. Stir until cornstarch is dissolved and set aside. In a medium saucepan over medium heat, combine sugar, vinegar, ketchup, soy sauce and salt. Once the mixture is simmering, stir in the pineapple juice mixture and stir constantly until the sauce is thickened. Pour the sauce evenly over the pork chops, vegetables and pineapple. Bake for 25-30 minutes, or until an inserted thermometer reaches 150 degrees F.

Serve pork chops with the vegetables, pineapple and the sauce drizzled over the top.

Shredded Sweet Pork Tacos

Where I live, there is a super popular Baja Mexican restaurant that fills their burritos, enchiladas and tacos with a shredded sweet pork. It is to die for. But, being who I am, I needed to meddle around a bit and figure out my own version. I wanted a little less sweet, a little more spicy and a touch of smoke. These tacos are just what I had in mind, the kind of thing where I took the first bite and groaned, smiled and high-fived myself in one motion. Have leftovers? Get creative! I always like to put the leftovers in quesadillas for lunch the next day.

Yields 6 servings

2 tablespoons extra virgin olive oil

1 yellow onion, diced

1 teaspoon kosher salt

½ teaspoon ground pepper

½ teaspoon dried oregano

2 bay leaves

6 garlic cloves, minced

3 tablespoons tomato paste

2 15-ounce cans crushed tomatoes

½ cup brown sugar

2 tablespoons honey

1 chipotle pepper in adobo sauce, seeded and minced

2 teaspoons adobo sauce from the chipotle pepper can

3 pounds boneless pork shoulder roast, cut in half lengthwise

In a large skillet over medium heat, add olive oil. Once the oil is heated, add the onion, salt, pepper, oregano and bay leaves. Saute until the onions are softened, about 10 minutes. Add the garlic and tomato paste and saute until tomato paste is broken up and the onions take on the red color. Stir in the tomatoes, brown sugar, honey, chipotle pepper and adobo sauce. Stir well and simmer for 5 minutes. Add both pieces of pork on top of the sauce. Cover the pan and simmer for 1 hour. Turn the pork over, reduce the heat to medium low and cover. Simmer for an additional hour, until pork is very tender and an inserted thermometer reaches 170 degrees F.

Remove pork from the sauce and set aside to cool. Once cool enough to handle, shred the pork into bite-sized pieces and put back into the sauce. Toss the pork with the sauce until the pork is well coated. Serve pork in tortillas with preferred toppings.

Shredded Sweet Pork Tacos
Refried Beans, Pg. 187
Mexican Rice, Pg. 188

Seafood

Roasted Hoisin Ginger Salmon 77

Cornmeal-Crusted Tilapia with Avocado Sauce 78

Tuna & Noodles 81

Shrimp Tacos with Creamy Chipotle Sauce 82

Baked Whole Trout with Lemon and Dill 85

Parchment Halibut with Zucchini, 86
Tomatoes & Spicy Creme Fraiche

Baked Halibut Fish Sticks with Tartar Sauce 89

Yellow Rice with Shrimp & Smoked Sausage 90

Grilled Bacon-Wrapped Shrimp 93

Pan-Seared Salmon with Warm Mango Salsa 94

Roasted Hoisin Ginger Salmon

Here are some perfectly paired flavors made to let salmon shine. Fresh ginger and sweet hoisin sauce make this salmon delicious as it is simple. Mix up the marinade in the afternoon and then let it sit until supper time. Why the afternoon and not morning? Seafood is a bit delicate and we don't want it falling apart due to a lengthy marinade, so let's keep it below 6 hours, okay?

Yields 6 servings.

¼ cup hoisin sauce

¼ cup soy sauce

3 tablespoons vegetable oil

2 tablespoons fresh lemon juice

2 tablespoons fresh ginger, grated

4 garlic cloves, minced

1 teaspoon ground pepper

6 salmon fillet portions

In a medium bowl, combine hoisin sauce, soy sauce, vegetable oil, lemon juice, ginger, garlic and pepper. Whisk well until combined. Pour mixture into a large zip seal bag. Add salmon portions and squish around so that each salmon portion is coated in marinade. Put in the fridge and let marinate for at least 1 hour or up to 6 hours.

Preheat oven to 375 degrees F. Spray a large baking sheet with non-stick spray. Place salmon portions on baking sheet, about 2 inches apart. Discard marinade. Cook for 18-20 minutes, until salmon is cooked through and flakes easily with a fork. Transfer a serving platter.

Cornmeal-Crusted Tilapia with Avocado Sauce

The avocado sauce is what makes this super creamy and full of flavor. You could slap this stuff on just about anything. As for the fish, it's crisp and moist. A quick sear in the pan ensures that it isn't dried out. Leftovers? I think one of these fillets would be delightful in a sandwich the next day.

Yields 6 servings

For the fish:
1 cup cornmeal
1½ teaspoons kosher salt
1 teaspoon ground pepper
½ teaspoon garlic powder
½ teaspoon paprika
6 tilapia fillets
4 tablespoons extra virgin olive oil, divided

For the sauce:
4 avocados
1½ teaspoons red wine vinegar
1½ teaspoons Worcestershire sauce
1 teaspoon kosher salt
2 garlic cloves
¼ cup cilantro leaves
Juice of 1 lime
¼ cup water

In a shallow dish, like a pie pan, combine cornmeal, salt, pepper, garlic powder and paprika. Whisk well to combine. Dredge each tilapia fillet in the cornmeal mixture, pressing it on to adhere.

In a large skillet over medium-high heat, add 2 tablespoons olive oil. Once the oil is heated, add three tilapia fillets. Sear on both sides until the fish is cooked through, about 3 minutes. Remove tilapia from the pan, onto a plate and cover with foil to keep warm. Repeat with the remaining fish and olive oil.

Once all the fish is cooked, make the sauce. In a blender, combine all sauce ingredients. Blend until smooth, adding more water if necessary to reach desired consistency.

Serve fish with a spoonful of sauce over the top.

Tuna & Noodles

I dare you to find someone who doesn't find this dish complete comfort food. It's nostalgic for some as well. For me, I remember resting a big bowl of this on my big pregnant belly, just a few weeks before my first son's arrival. Something about the chunks of tuna, tender noodles and creamy sauce helped me forget my swollen feet and achy back.

Yields 8 servings

2 tablespoons unsalted butter
½ yellow onion, diced
1 celery stalk, diced
8 ounces white mushrooms, sliced
2 garlic cloves, minced
1½ teaspoons kosher salt
1 teaspoon ground pepper
¼ cup all-purpose flour

2½ cups milk
1 cup frozen green peas
2 5-ounce cans tuna fish, drained
12 ounces wide egg noodles, cooked according to package directions
1 cup panko breadcrumbs
½ teaspoon kosher salt
2 tablespoons unsalted butter, melted

Preheat oven to 400 degrees F.

In a large skillet over medium-high heat, add butter. Once butter is melted, add onion, celery, mushrooms, garlic, salt and pepper. Saute until vegetables are softened, about 10 minutes. Reduce heat to medium and add flour, mixing well to combine with the vegetables. Saute for an additional 5 minutes. Pour in milk and simmer, stirring occasionally, until mixture is thickened, about 5 minutes. Stir in peas, tuna fish and cooked egg noodles. Mix well to combine. Pour noodle mixture into a 9x13 inch pan and spread evenly.

In a small bowl, combine bread crumbs, salt and butter. Mix until bread crumbs are moistened. Sprinkle breadcrumbs over the noodle mixture. Bake for 15-20 minutes, or until the bread crumbs are lightly toasted.

Shrimp Tacos with Creamy Chipotle Sauce

This right here is the way to my heart. I love me some great Baja Mexican food. I love the fresh, simple flavors. I love how laid back it seems. No fuss. This recipe is something made in our home often, mostly because I am the one doing the cooking and I am a bit of a dictator when it comes to the kitchen. It is a good thing this is a big hit with all my family. Besides being delicious, these tacos can be on the table in less than 30 minutes.

Yields 6 servings

For the tacos:
1 pound medium shrimp, peeled, deveined and tails removed
3 garlic cloves, minced
1 teaspoon ground cumin
½ teaspoon ground pepper
½ teaspoon kosher salt
¼ teaspoon chile powder
2 tablespoons extra virgin olive oil
2 teaspoons fresh lime juice
6 warm corn tortillas
2 cups shredded savoy cabbage

For the sauce:
¼ cup mayonnaise
¼ cup plain yogurt
1 chipotle pepper, seeded and finely minced
½ teaspoon adobo sauce from the chipotle pepper can

In a small bowl, combine all sauce ingredients and whisk well. Set aside.

Prepare the tacos. In a large bowl, combine the shrimp, garlic, cumin, pepper, salt and chile powder. Toss well until all the shrimp are coated. Let marinate for 15 minutes.

In a large skillet over medium high-heat, heat olive oil. Once the oil is ready, add the shrimp. Saute, stirring often, until shrimp are cooked through, about 5-8 minutes. Remove pan from heat, pour lime juice over the shrimp and toss well to combine.

Serve shrimp in a tortilla with shredded cabbage and a spoonful of the creamy chipotle sauce.

Baked Whole Trout with Lemon & Dill
Toasted Couscous with Leeks & Garlic, Pg. 189

Baked Whole Trout with Lemon & Dill

This is the perfect example of keeping it easy. Whole fish stuffed with lemon and dill, and simply seasoned with salt and pepper. Nothing too complex, just clean flavors that allow the fish to shine. This trout also provides a little show at the table. After the fish is cooked and on the serving platter, you remove the fish heads and skin at the table. Don't stress; it's easy! The heads and skin pull right off once they are cooked. If you are weird and disgusting like my kids, you fight over who gets to eat the fish eyeballs. Sometimes, I truly wonder if I really gave birth to my three crazies.

Yields 6 servings

3 whole trout, cleaned
Extra virgin olive oil, for seasoning
Kosher salt and ground pepper, for seasoning
2 lemons, sliced
1 bunch fresh baby dill

Preheat oven to 425 degrees F. Spray a baking sheet with non-stick spray. Rinse fish inside and out, and dry. Rub a small amount of olive oil onto each fish on the outside and inside, then season with salt and pepper on the outside and inside. Evenly divide the lemon and dill between the fish and stuff each of them. Lay them on the prepared baking sheet and bake for 20 minutes, until cooked through.

Transfer baked trout to a serving platter. At the table, with a fork, gently remove the fish heads and peel the skin off. Carefully pull the fish halves apart and remove the bones. Discard dill and lemon slices.

Parchment Halibut with Zucchini, Tomatoes & Spicy Creme Fraiche

Anything in parchment always feels special, like a little present on your dinner plate. This little present is a surprise of tender halibut and fresh summer vegetables topped with a creamy, spicy sauce. And dinner clean up has never been easier. No halibut? No problem. Just use whatever white fish looks good at the grocery store.

Yields 6 servings

For the halibut:
6 halibut fillet portions
Kosher salt and ground pepper, for seasoning
6 tablespoons butter, divided
2 small zucchini, thinly sliced
30 cherry tomatoes, halved

For the creme fraiche:
1 8-ounce tub of creme fraiche
2 teaspoons Sriracha hot sauce
½ teaspoon kosher salt

Set oven to 400 degrees F. Tear off six 18 inch pieces of parchment paper and set them aside.

Set one halibut portion onto a sheet of parchment. Season with salt and pepper. Place 1 tablespoon butter on top. Lay a small handful of zucchini slices on top and ten cherry tomato halves. Bring up the long sides of the parchment and fold down all the way to the fish. Fold up the sides, staple shut with an office stapler and set on a baking sheet. Parchment packet does not need to be airtight, but it does need to be snug. Repeat with remaining fish and vegetables.

Bake parchment pouches for 15 minutes, until fish is cooked through and vegetables are tender.

While the halibut bakes, make the spicy creme fraiche. In a medium bowl, combine creme fraiche, Sriracha and salt. Mix well and set aside.

To serve, set parchment pouches on plates and gently rip open to release heat. Spoon a dollop of the spicy creme fraiche onto the fish. Eat right out of the parchment.

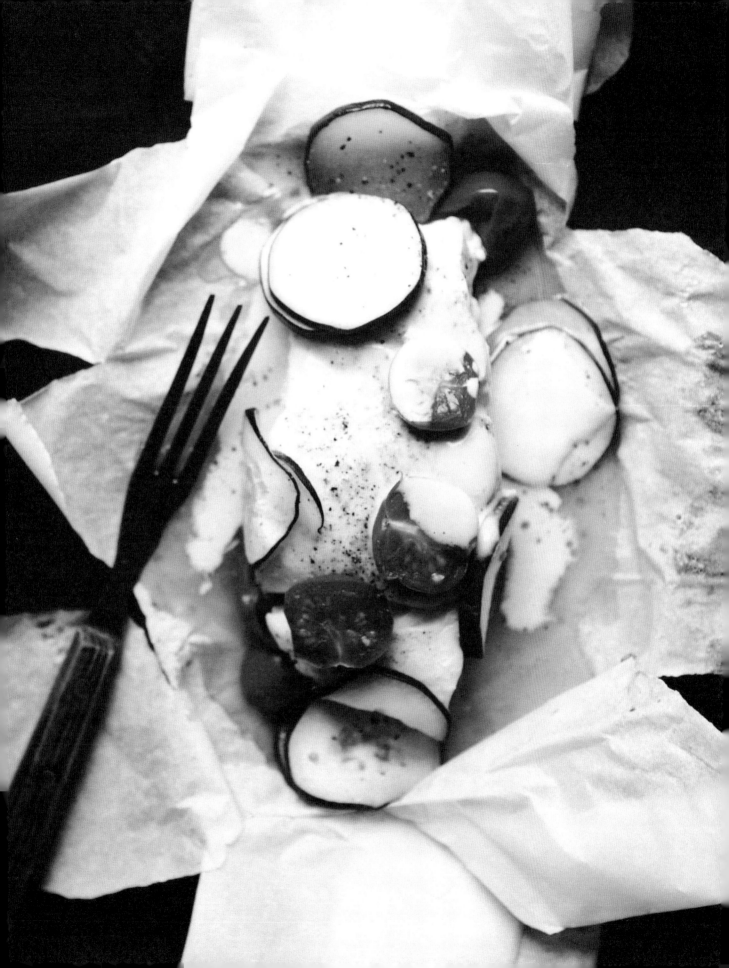

Baked Halibut Fish Sticks with Tartar Sauce

Kid food elevated. No minced mystery fish here! Big chunks of halibut, breaded in panko bread crumbs and lemon zest, then dipped in the most delicious homemade tartar sauce. Excellent as an appetizer or an entree. Whoever it is that you serve this to will be grateful for the grown-up version of a food, too often done wrong, finally done right.

Yields 6 servings

For the sauce:
1 cup mayonnaise
3 tablespoons dill pickle relish
2 teaspoons fresh lemon juice
½ teaspoon dijon mustard
½ teaspoon Worcestershire sauce
½ teaspoon kosher salt

For the fish:
2½ pounds halibut fillets, skinned and cut into ¾ inch strips
2 eggs, beaten
2 teaspoons water
2 cups panko bread crumbs
1 lemon, zested
2 teaspoons kosher salt
½ teaspoon ground pepper
Lemon wedges, for serving

Preheat oven to 475 degrees F.

In a medium bowl, combine all sauce ingredients. Mix well to combine and set in the refrigerator to chill.

In a shallow dish, like a pie pan, combine eggs and water. In another shallow dish, combine panko bread crumbs, lemon zest, salt and pepper. Mix well, being sure to evenly distribute lemon zest.

Set up a breading station. In order, line up the fish, egg mixture, panko bread crumb mixture and a large plate. With one piece at a time, dip the fish in the egg first, then into the panko bread crumb mixture, coating well, and then onto the plate. Repeat until all fish sticks are breaded.

Set a baking sheet in the preheated oven. Let it sit and get hot for 5 minutes. Remove hot pan from the oven and immediately spray with non-stick spray. Set fish on the hot pan in a single layer. Bake for 10 minutes, or until the fish sticks are lightly browned and opaque all the way through. Serve with tartar sauce and lemon wedges.

Yellow Rice with Shrimp & Smoked Sausage

This is a lot like a Spanish paella. Let's call this a cheater paella. It has lots of the classic flavors in a paella, just not the same technique. We have loads of flavor going on here. Shrimp, smoked sausage, onions, garlic and then gorgeous color with saffron. This here is one of those one-pot meals, and who doesn't like that? I think all you would need would be a big hunk of crusty bread to scoop up the rice.

Yields 6 servings

2 tablespoons extra virgin olive oil
1 yellow onion, diced
1 red bell pepper, diced
4 garlic cloves, minced
1 teaspoon kosher salt
½ teaspoon ground pepper
2 cups basmati rice
3 cups low-sodium chicken stock

⅛ teaspoon crushed red pepper flakes
¼ teaspoon saffron, crushed
1 bay leaf
1 pound smoked sausage, sliced
1 pound medium shrimp, peeled and deveined
1 tablespoon chopped fresh parsley
Lemon wedges, for serving

In a large pot over medium-high heat, add olive oil. Once the oil is heated, add onion, bell pepper, garlic, salt and pepper. Saute until vegetables are softened, about 10 minutes. Add rice and stir until combined. Turn heat to high and pour in chicken stock. Once boiling, add red pepper flakes, saffron and bay leaf. Stir in smoked sausage, cover and reduce heat to low. Simmer for 15 minutes, stir and then add shrimp in a single layer on top. Cover and simmer for an additional 10 minutes.

Transfer rice into a serving bowl. Remove bay leaf. Garnish with parsley and lemon wedges.

Grilled Bacon-Wrapped Shrimp

In the words of a popular character on "Parks and Recreation," this is my second favorite food wrapped around my third favorite food. My favorite foods are first chocolate, then bacon and then shrimp. I could dip these tasty shrimp in chocolate, but that is going a little too far, don't you think? These are simple to make; they just require a little more hands on time than most recipes. You first cook the bacon, but undercook it, just so it renders some fat, but not all of it. Then wrap it around shrimp, slide it onto a skewer and grill. As they grill, dab on a bit of barbecue sauce and you're done!

Yields 6 servings

18 pieces bacon, cut in half crosswise
36 medium shrimp, peeled, deveined with tails left on
Kosher salt, for seasoning
1½ cups barbecue, store-bought or homemade
6 skewers, metal and wooden

In a large skillet over medium high heat, add a few strips of bacon. Cook, flipping over once, until bacon is lightly browned on the edges and some of the fat has rendered, but do not cook all the way through. Set aside on a paper towel-lined plate. Repeat with remaining bacon. Once all bacon is cooked, wrap one piece of bacon around one shrimp. Thread six bacon-wrapped shrimp onto a skewer. Repeat with remaining shrimp.

Heat grill to medium-high. Once hot, add skewers. Dab barbecue sauce onto the shrimp. Once bacon starts to crisp, flip over and dab barbecue sauce onto the cooked side. When bacon has crisped on the other side, flip over and grill for 30 seconds, just until barbecue sauce is caramelized. Serve warm.

Pan-Seared Salmon with Warm Mango Salsa

Salmon and mango, two things you can never go wrong with. Here, they combine for a healthy, sleek dinner entree. And it is incredibly easy. Mango brings fruity sweetness and salmon brings bold seafood flavor. This delish dish is a feast for the eyes with all the bright yellow, green and pink. It's perfect for you food porn addicts.

Yields 6 servings

For the salsa:
2 mangos, diced
2 jalapenos, seeded and diced
1 seedless cucumber, diced
1/2 red onion, diced
1/2 cup fresh cilantro, minced
1/4 cup fresh lime juice
4 teaspoons honey
1 teaspoon kosher salt
1/2 teaspoon chile powder

For the salmon:
6 salmon portions
Kosher salt and ground pepper, for seasoning
2 tablespoons extra virgin olive oil
Lime wedges, for serving

In a medium bowl, combine all salsa ingredients. Mix well until combined and set aside.

Season the salmon with salt and pepper on both sides. In a large skillet over medium-high heat, add olive oil. Once the oil is heated, add three salmon portions, skin side down. Sear until skin is crisp and the salmon begins to cook on the edges, about 3 minutes. Flip over and sear until salmon is cooked through, about 3 minutes. Set salmon onto a serving platter and set aside. Repeat with the remaining salmon. Once all salmon is cooked, reduce heat to medium and pour in mango salsa. Saute, stirring well, until salsa is hot, about 2 minutes. Pour salsa over the salmon on the serving platter.

Vegetarian

Black Bean Burgers 99

Zucchini & Bell Pepper Enchiladas 100

Black Beans and Rice 103

Vegetable Egg Rolls 104

Grilled Vegetable Tacos 107

Grilled Flatbread with Goat Cheese, 108
Roasted Red Peppers and Fennel

Spinach Artichoke Turnovers 111

Eggplant & Chickpea Curry 112

Baked Eggs with Chard & Feta Cheese 115

Grilled Tomato & Onion Crostinis with Basil Oil 116

Black Bean Burgers
Sauteed Corn with Lime & Queso Fresco, Pg. 184

Black Bean Burgers

Vegetarianism never tasted so good! Who would have thought those cans of black beans could become such a standout favorite? Treat these like any regular burger when you start adding toppings. Have a few leftover patties? How about an over easy egg on top of one for breakfast?

Yields 6 burgers

2 15-ounce cans black beans, drained and rinsed
6 tablespoons extra virgin olive oil, divided
½ red onion, diced
1 teaspoon kosher salt
1½ teaspoons dried oregano
1 teaspoon ground cumin
½ teaspoon ground pepper
½ teaspoon fresh lime juice
4 garlic cloves, minced
¼ cup plain bread crumbs
6 hamburger buns, for serving

Add the beans to a large bowl and mash with a masher or your hands. Set aside.

In a small skillet over medium heat, add 2 tablespoons olive oil. Once oil is heated, add onions and salt and saute until softened, stirring occasionally, for about 10 minutes. Add to black beans. Add oregano, cumin, pepper, lime juice, garlic and bread crumbs. Stir well to combine. Divide black bean mixture into 6 portions and shape each portion into a patty and set aside.

In a large skillet over medium-high heat, add 2 tablespoons olive oil. Once oil is heated, add three patties and sear on each side for 3-5 minutes, until a crust forms. Repeat with the remaining olive oil and patties.

Assemble cooked burgers with your preferred toppings.

Zucchini & Bell Pepper Enchiladas

You won't miss the meat in this dish. These enchiladas are filled with colorful vegetables, all lending their diverse flavors: sweet, spicy, savory, smoky. These are ideal for when your summer garden is at it's peak. I especially love this recipe for the tortilla trick I learned from my friend Elizabeth. Instead of softening the tortillas in hot oil before rolling, dip them in hot water and you will get the same soft result, minus the extra fat.

Yields 6 servings

2 tablespoons extra virgin olive oil
1 red bell pepper, thinly sliced
½ yellow onion, thinly sliced
1 teaspoon kosher salt
1 cup corn, fresh or frozen
1 medium zucchini, shredded
1 Anaheim chile, seeded and minced

2 garlic cloves, minced
½ teaspoon ground cumin
1 large tomato, chopped
10 corn tortillas
2 cups shredded Monterey Jack cheese
1 15-ounce can red enchilada sauce

In a large skillet over medium-high heat, add the olive oil. Once the oil is heated, add the bell peppers, onions and salt. Saute until softened and the peppers are slightly charred, about 10 minutes. Add the corn, zucchini, chile, garlic and cumin. Stir until combined and saute until zucchini and corn are softened, about 3 minutes. Stir in tomatoes. Cook for 3 more minutes and remove pan from heat.

Preheat oven to 375 degrees F.

Fill a medium saucepan with water and set over high heat. Bring to a boil, then set heat to low. Spoon a small amount of enchilada sauce into a 9x13 inch pan, enough to cover the bottom. Dip a tortilla in the simmering water for 3 seconds, remove and pat dry. Spoon in ⅓ cup of zucchini and bell pepper mixture and roll up the tortilla. Place in pan seam side down. Repeat with remaining filling and tortillas.

Pour remaining enchilada sauce over the top and sprinkle on the shredded cheese.
Bake for 15-20 minutes, or until cheese is melted.

Black Beans & Rice

This is a go-to meal in our house. It has such simple, delicious flavors. I usually have all the ingredients on hand, and this is happily consumed by all my people. This also works great in a Thermos the next day for my son's lunch at school.

Yields 6 servings

2 tablespoons extra virgin olive oil

1 yellow onion, diced

1 green bell pepper, diced

5 garlic cloves, minced

1 teaspoon kosher salt

2 15-ounce cans black beans, drained and rinsed

1 15-ounce can diced tomatoes, undrained

2 cups vegetable stock

1 bay leaf

½ teaspoon ground cumin

½ teaspoon dried oregano

⅛ teaspoon chile powder

2 teaspoons lime juice

2 tablespoons chopped fresh cilantro

1½ cups long grain rice, cooked according to package directions

In a large skillet over medium high heat, add olive oil. Once oil is heated, add onion, green bell pepper, garlic and salt. Saute until onion and bell pepper are softened, about 10 minutes. Stir in black beans, tomatoes, vegetable stock, bay leaf, cumin, oregano and chile powder. Simmer, stirring occasionally, for 20 minutes, until most of the liquid has evaporated. Remove bay leaf and stir in lime juice and cilantro.

Serve black beans over rice.

Vegetable Egg Rolls

This is a dish you can get the whole family helping with. Let them do the work of rolling the egg rolls while you fry them. These produce crisp, golden egg rolls filled with vegetables and flavored with fresh ginger and garlic. Don't want to fry all of them? Go ahead put them in a freezer bag and throw them in the freezer and fry another time.

Yields 6 servings

2 tablespoons vegetable oil

2 14-ounce bags or 12 cups shredded green cabbage

2 ounces snow peas, roughly chopped

2 cups mung bean sprouts

1 cup shredded carrots

2 teaspoons grated fresh ginger

4 garlic cloves, minced

¼ cup soy sauce

4 teaspoons rice vinegar

2 teaspoons sesame oil

2 teaspoons sesame seeds

1 teaspoon kosher salt

26 egg roll wrappers

48-ounce bottle vegetable oil, for frying

In a large skillet over medium-high heat, add vegetable oil. Once oil is heated, add cabbage, snow peas, mung bean sprouts, carrots, ginger and garlic. Toss gently to combine. Saute for 10 minutes, until cabbage is cooked down and softened. Stir in soy sauce, rice vinegar, sesame oil, sesame seeds and salt. Stir occasionally until most liquid is absorbed, about 5 minutes. Transfer cabbage mixture to a strainer and let all the liquid drain. Let cabbage mixture cool completely.

Line a baking sheet with paper towels. Pour vegetable oil into a large pot or electric skillet. Heat oil to 375 degrees. While oil is heating, set one egg roll wrapper onto your workspace. Put two tablespoons of cabbage mixture in the middle of the wrapper. Fold the bottom corner over the top. Roll up once and then fold in the sides. Roll all the way and set on the prepared baking sheet. Repeat with the remaining filling and wrappers. Keep a damp towel over the egg roll wrappers until they are used.

Gently drop three egg rolls into the hot oil. Fry until golden and crisp, about 5 minutes. Set fried egg rolls onto a paper towel lined baking sheet and let cool. Repeat with remaining egg rolls. Serve egg rolls with soy sauce or sweet chile sauce for dipping.

Grilled Vegetable Tacos
Guacamole, Pg. 178

Grilled Vegetable Tacos

I think it is quite possible that a vegetable reaches its pinnacle of glory when it is grilled. All that natural sweetness is exposed and the vegetables get a delicious char on them. Wrap all those veggies in a tortilla, slather on some guac (pg. 178) and you are experiencing vegetables at their best.

Yields 6 servings

1 teaspoon kosher salt
½ teaspoon garlic powder
½ teaspoon ground cumin
¼ teaspoon chile powder

2 ears corn, shucked, silks removed and cut in half lengthwise

3 medium zucchini, sliced lengthwise into thick strips

2 red bell peppers, sliced lengthwise into thick strips

4 portabella mushrooms, sliced into thick strips

3 tablespoons extra virgin olive oil
6 flour tortillas
2 tablespoons chopped fresh cilantro
1 lime, cut into wedges, for serving

Heat grill to medium-high. In a small bowl, combine salt, garlic powder, cumin and chile powder. Mix well and set aside.

In a large bowl, combine corn, zucchini, bell pepper, mushroom and olive oil. Toss well, coating all vegetables in olive oil. Sprinkle salt mixture over the top and toss again to combine.

Pour vegetables onto the grill and grill covered for 5 minutes. Turn vegetables, cover again and grill for an additional 5 minutes. Transfer vegetables to a serving platter. Turn heat on the grill up to high and grill tortillas on both sides until charred, about 2 minutes. Set tortillas on a plate and cover with a towel and set aside.

Carefully cut corn kernels off the cobs and add them to the serving platter. Sprinkle cilantro on top of grilled vegetables. Serve vegetables with charred tortillas and lime wedges.

Grilled Flatbread with Goat Cheese, Roasted Red Peppers & Fennel

My darn food photographer Sheena, was adamant that I would like goat cheese if it was on grilled flatbread. She insisted I try it. So with her in mind, I developed a recipe for that very thing. With much hesitation and doubt, I pressed forward with my flavor ideas, truly wondering if Sheena could be right. Goat cheese smells terrible, so how could it possibly taste decent? Well, what do you know, she was right! The bright flavors of the fennel and roasted red peppers really stand out with the creamy goat cheese. I think this means I might like goat cheese now!

Yields 4 servings

1 cup hot water
1 .25 ounce packet active dry yeast
2 ¾ cups all-purpose flour
1 teaspoon kosher salt

1 7-ounce package goat cheese
1 cup diced roasted red peppers
1 fennel bulb, thinly sliced
Extra virgin olive oil, for seasoning

In a small bowl, combine hot water and yeast. Let sit for 10 minutes, until yeast is dissolved.

In a mixer fitted with a kneading attachment, combine flour and 1 teaspoon salt. Mix until combined. Pour in yeast mixture and mix on medium until dough forms a ball. Reduce speed to low and continue mixing to knead for 5 minutes. Remove dough from dough hook, form into a ball, spray the inside of the bowl with non-stick spray and set the dough back into the mixing bowl. Cover the bowl with a towel and set it in a warm place. Let rise for 45 minutes to an hour, until dough doubles in size.

Once dough has risen, spray counter top with non-stick spray. Divide the dough into four portions. Roll each dough portion out to ½ inch thick. Heat grill to high and with the grill uncovered, grill each flatbread on one side, until grill marks appear, about 3 minutes. Remove from the grill and on the grilled side, crumble ¼ of the goat cheese evenly over each flatbread. Next add ¼ cup roasted red peppers and a few slices of fennel. Grill each flatbread on uncooked side, with the grill covered, until vegetables are slightly charred and flatbread is cooked through, about 5 minutes.

Before serving, drizzle olive oil over each flatbread.

Grilled Flatbread with Goat Cheese,
Roasted Red Peppers & Fennel

Cantaloupe Agua Fresca, Pg. 245

Grilled Tomato and Onion Crostinis
with Basil Oil, Pg. 116

Spinach Artichoke Turnovers

This husband of mine, he is one dynamite guy. Besides having the husband/father thing down, he is also a whiz in the kitchen, which is convenient when owning a catering company. One dish he is asked to do over and over again, no matter how passe it may be, is spinach artichoke dip. His clients can't get their fill. Here, we took his spinach artichoke dip, tweaked it slightly and wrapped it in buttery puff pastry. It's almost better than the dip itself.

Yields 8 servings

1 8-ounce package cream cheese, softened

2 cups fresh baby spinach leaves

2 6.5-ounce jars marinated artichoke hearts, drained and roughly chopped

1 cup shredded mozzarella cheese

¼ cup shredded parmesan cheese

2 garlic cloves, minced

1 tablespoon extra virgin olive oil

½ teaspoon kosher salt

¼ teaspoon ground pepper

2 sheets puff pastry, thawed

1 egg

Preheat the oven to 400 degrees F.

In a large bowl, combine cream cheese, spinach, artichoke hearts, mozzarella, parmesan, garlic, olive oil, salt and pepper. Mix until combined, squeezing the cream cheese to break it up. Once well combined, set aside.

On a lightly floured surface, spread out one puff pastry sheet. With a knife, cut the sheet into four triangles, corner to corner. In the middle of one triangle, add ¼ cup of the spinach artichoke mixture. Fold the triangle in half, covering the spinach/artichoke mixture. With a fork, press all around the edges to seal it. Set onto a baking sheet and repeat with the remaining puff pastry triangles.

In a small bowl, combine egg and 1 teaspoon of water. Whisk until combined. With a pastry brush, brush the tops of each turnover with the egg mixture.

Bake for 15-18 minutes, or until the tops are lightly browned.

Eggplant & Chickpea Curry

This is a treat I hoard for myself. Well, actually, let's be honest. I don't have to hoard it. My kids aren't huge fans of curry and eggplant. But just in case they get a wild hair, I keep this tucked away in the fridge and have it last all week for my lunch. Curry gets better as the days go by. Flavors develop and burrow deeper into the vegetables. Nobody likes being a leftover more than curry. And curry seems to taste even better with some rain or snow falling outside. Spices warming you up from the inside out. Oh! And P.S., this is vegan!

Yields 6 servings

1 large eggplant
2 tablespoons extra virgin olive oil
½ red bell pepper, diced
½ yellow onion, diced
½ teaspoon kosher salt
1 garlic clove, minced
1½ teaspoons grated fresh ginger
1¼ teaspoons ground coriander
1 teaspoon ground cumin

½ teaspoon turmeric
1 15-ounce can diced tomatoes
1 15-ounce can chickpeas, drained and rinsed
½ cup water
¼ teaspoon garam masala
2 tablespoons minced fresh cilantro
1½ cups basmati rice, prepared according to package directions.

Preheat oven to 400 degrees F. Poke the eggplant all over with a fork and set on a baking sheet. Roast eggplant for 40-45 minutes, until the center is soft. Set aside until cool enough to handle. Once cooled, peel off the skin and cut into small chunks. Set aside.

In a large skillet over medium heat, add olive oil. Once oil is heated, add red bell pepper, onion and salt. Saute until vegetables are softened, about 10 minutes. Stir in garlic, ginger, coriander, cumin and turmeric. Stir well and saute until fragrant, about 5 minutes. Stir in cooked eggplant, tomatoes, chickpeas and water. Simmer for 10 minutes, or until the water is mostly evaporated. Stir in garam masala and cilantro. Serve over basmati rice.

Baked Eggs with Chard & Feta Cheese

Eggs are not just for breakfast! Repeat with me: Eggs are not just for breakfast! They are also for dinner and they are lovely with some healthful greens. The onions and peppers in this make for a bit of sweetness, and the cheese brings in some tanginess. This dish comes together in 20 minutes, and it is super satisfying. Put this on your weekly menu quick!

Yields 6 servings

2 tablespoons extra virgin olive oil
½ yellow onion, diced
½ red bell pepper, diced
1 teaspoon kosher salt
½ teaspoon ground pepper
3 garlic cloves, minced
12 cups chopped fresh red chard
6 eggs
¼ cup crumbled feta cheese

Set oven to 400 degrees.

In a large, oven-proof skillet over medium heat, add olive oil. Once oil is heated, add onion, red bell pepper, salt and pepper. Saute until vegetables are softened, about 10 minutes. Once vegetables are softened, add garlic and saute for one additional minute. Add chard and saute until chard is wilted down, about 2 minutes. Remove pan from the heat and make six small wells in the chard. Crack one egg into each well. Season the top of each egg with salt and pepper. Sprinkle on feta cheese. Set the pan in the oven and bake for 5-10 minutes, depending on the desired doneness of your eggs.

To serve, scoop up an egg with some of the chard.

Grilled Tomato & Onion Crostinis with Basil Oil

This is the perfect way to showcase summer. A grill, garden veggies and a bright green drizzle on top are all you need. This and a cold drink could make anyone happy. Serve these as an appetizer or as a main dish. If you have any leftover basil oil, toss it with some pasta the next day for a light, easy dinner.

Yields 8 servings

For the oil:
3 cups fresh basil leaves
½ cup extra virgin olive oil
1 teaspoon balsamic vinegar
1 teaspoon kosher salt
1 garlic clove

For the crostinis:
8 ½-inch thick french bread slices
2 tablespoons extra virgin olive oil
Kosher salt, for seasoning
8 ½-inch thick red onion slices
8 ½-inch thick tomato slices

In a blender, add basil leaves, olive oil, balsamic vinegar, kosher salt and garlic clove. Blend on high until basil leaves are broken up and sauce is smooth. Pour basil oil into a small bowl and set aside.

After the oil is made, make the crostinis. Heat grill to high. Set french bread slices onto a serving platter. Pour 2 tablespoons olive oil into a small bowl and brush both sides of the bread with a pastry brush. Sprinkle each side with a small amount of kosher salt.

Set the bread slices and the onion slices on the grill. Grill the bread on each side until toasted and grill marks appear, about 3 minutes on each side. Remove bread slices and set onto the serving platter. Add the tomatoes and continue to grill with the onions until grill marks appear, about 5 minutes on each side. Remove tomato slices and set one on each slice of bread. Add the onions on top of the tomatoes. Drizzle each crostini with basil oil and serve.

Pictured on Page 109.

Notes

Pasta & Polenta

Crispy Polenta with Sausage & Fresh Tomato Ragu 121

Farfalle with Pumpkin Cream Sauce & Bacon 122

Spaghetti with Marinara Sauce 125

Baked Penne with Sausage, Spinach & Red Bell Peppers 126

Fetuccine with Tomato Cream Sauce 129

Sausage & Bacon Lasagna 130

Penne with Beans & Arugula Pesto 133

Crispy Polenta with Sausage & Fresh Tomato Ragu

Liven up your pasta routine with this dish. Crisp polenta smothered in a chunky sauce full of fresh tomatoes and plenty of Italian sausage. Polenta can also be made beforehand and then livened up with a quick crisp in a skillet later. This is a great meal for you people that like to get dinner made ahead of time.

Yields 6 servings

For the polenta:

3 cups water

1 cup polenta

½ teaspoon kosher salt

2 tablespoons unsalted butter

¼ cup shredded Parmesan cheese

For the ragu:

5 sweet Italian sausage links, casings removed

½ yellow onion, diced

1 carrot, peeled and diced

1 celery stalk, diced

2 garlic cloves, minced

1 teaspoon kosher salt

2 tablespoons tomato paste

2½ pounds tomatoes, about 10 tomatoes, diced

3 tablespoons extra virgin olive oil, for crisping polenta

Spray an 8x8 inch pan with non-stick spray and set aside.

In a large pot over high heat, add water and bring to a boil. Once boiling, slowly stir in polenta and ½ teaspoon salt. Reduce heat to low and stir polenta occasionally for 30 minutes, until all water is absorbed and polenta is thick and soft to the bite. Stir in butter and Parmesan cheese. Once butter is melted, transfer polenta to the prepared pan. Smooth the top, cover with plastic and put polenta in the refrigerator to cool.

While the polenta cools, make the ragu. In a large skillet over medium-high heat, add sausage, onion, carrot, celery, garlic and salt. Saute, breaking up the sausage, until vegetables are softened and sausage is cooked through, about 10 minutes. Add tomato paste and saute until vegetables and sausage take on the red color of the paste. Stir in tomatoes, reduce heat to medium and cover. Simmer, stirring occasionally for 20 minutes, until tomatoes are broken down and have released their juices.

After the ragu is finished, remove the polenta from the fridge. Invert pan and remove the polenta. Cut polenta into nine squares. In a medium skillet over medium-high heat, add 1 tablespoon olive oil. Once the oil is heated, add three polenta squares. Fry on each side until crisp, about 2 minutes. Transfer the polenta on a plate and set aside. Repeat with last 2 tablespoons of olive oil and six polenta squares.

Serve sausage and fresh tomato ragu over crispy polenta squares.

Farfalle with Pumpkin Cream Sauce & Bacon

Pumpkin is a treasure trove of nutrients, so why not add it to something besides sweet quick bread or cookies? Let's make some dinner with it. It is a powerhouse of fiber and both vitamins A and E. It also contains alpha and beta carotene, both of which are major antioxidants. So while this pasta is rich with cream and bacon, take comfort in the nutrients from the pumpkin. Big nutrients cancel out heavy cream, right?

Yields 6 servings

5 strips bacon, diced
½ yellow onion, diced
½ teaspoon kosher salt
½ teaspoon ground pepper
3 garlic cloves, minced
1 tablespoon minced fresh sage
1¼ cups heavy cream
1 cup canned pumpkin puree
¼ cup shredded fresh Parmesan cheese
1 pound farfalle pasta, cooked according to package directions

In a large skillet over medium-high heat, add bacon. Saute until bacon is cooked through and crisp. Remove bacon with a slotted spoon and set aside in a small bowl, leaving the bacon fat in the pan. Reduce heat to medium and add onion, salt and pepper. Saute until onion is softened, about 5 minutes. Add garlic and sage and saute for 1 additional minute. Stir in heavy cream, pumpkin puree and Parmesan cheese. Simmer for 5 minutes, until the pumpkin cream sauce has thickened. Pour sauce over pasta and toss until pasta is well coated. Transfer to a serving dish and garnish with the cooked bacon.

Spaghetti with Marinara Sauce

Here is a great last-minute meal staple to add to your list of what to make when dinner time seemingly crept up without notice. You probably have everything in your pantry at this moment. What makes this marinara better than anything in a jar? Fennel. Fennel seed is the secret. It adds a subtle sweetness that goes great with tomato. And hey, since you are already making one batch of marinara, might as well double it and make extra sauce to keep in the freezer.

Yields 6 servings

2 tablespoons extra virgin olive oil
1 yellow onion, diced
1 teaspoon kosher salt
½ teaspoon ground pepper
2 garlic cloves, minced
1 tablespoon tomato paste
1 15-ounce can diced tomatoes
2 15-ounce cans tomato sauce
1/2 cup water

2 teaspoons dried basil
1 teaspoon dried oregano
1 teaspoon dried thyme
¼ teaspoon fennel seed
⅛ teaspoon crushed red pepper flakes
1 pound spaghetti, cooked according to package directions
Shredded Parmesan cheese, for serving
Fresh minced basil, for serving

In a large skillet over medium heat, add olive oil. Once oil is heated, add the onion, salt and pepper. Saute until onion is softened, about 10 minutes. Add garlic and tomato paste and saute until the paste is broken up and the onions take on the red color. Pour in the diced tomatoes, tomato sauce and water. Stir in the basil, oregano, thyme, fennel seed and crushed red pepper flakes. Turn heat to medium low and simmer for 10 minutes.

Toss marinara sauce with cooked spaghetti. Garnish with Parmesan cheese and basil.

Baked Penne with Sausage, Spinach & Red Bell Peppers

Can I tell you what this is perfect for? It is the perfect dish to bring to a family with a brand new baby. It can feed a big group, it holds up as leftovers and it is a full meal in one pan. Meaty Italian sausage, tangy tomatoes, sweet bell peppers, bright green spinach and loads of melty, stretchy mozzarella. Come on! What new mama and her accompanying hungry family wouldn't love that?

Yields 8 servings

1 pound penne pasta
5 tablespoons extra virgin olive oil, divided
5 links mild Italian sausage, about 16 ounces
1 red bell pepper, diced
1 yellow onion, diced
1 teaspoon kosher salt
½ teaspoon ground pepper

1 teaspoon dried Italian seasoning blend
2 garlic cloves, minced
2 cups heavy cream
1½ cups shredded Parmesan cheese
4 Roma tomatoes, chopped
1 cup baby spinach leaves
4 cups shredded mozzarella cheese, divided

Preheat the oven to 450 degrees F.

Set a large pot of salted water over high heat and bring to a boil. Cook pasta until soft on the outside, but not cooked all the way through. Drain, pour back into pot and toss with 3 tablespoons olive oil. Set aside, stirring occasionally while preparing the other ingredients.

In a large skillet over medium heat, cook sausage links for 15 minutes, flipping once, until sausage is cooked through. Once cool enough to handle, slice sausage into ½ inch thick slices and set aside.

In the same skillet over medium-high heat, add remaining 2 tablespoons olive oil, red bell pepper, onion, salt, pepper and Italian seasoning. Saute until vegetables are softened, about 5 minutes. Add garlic and saute for 1 additional minute. Reduce heat to medium and stir in heavy cream and Parmesan cheese. Simmer for 8 to 10 minutes, until the cream sauce has thickened.

In the pasta pot, combine pasta, sausage, tomatoes, spinach and 3 cups mozzarella. Stir well to combine. Pour in cream sauce. Toss gently. Pour mixture into a 9x13 inch baking dish. Sprinkle reserved 1 cup mozzarella cheese on top. Bake for 20 minutes, until cheese is browned and pasta is cooked through.

Fettuccine with Tomato Cream Sauce

I have this little 2 year old who will eat pasta until the cows come home. She takes it by the handfuls and stuffs it into her hungry trap. She uses her chubby fingers to sop up the sauce then licks them clean. She takes no regard for pasta getting into her ringlet blond hair or all over her white onesie. You will never see a soul enjoy pasta more than she does. This is one pasta dish she prefers over all. A simple tangy cream sauce tossed with fettuccine and garnished with fresh basil. Enjoy, but don't get any in your hair.

Yields 6 servings

2 tablespoons unsalted butter
2 shallots, diced
2 garlic cloves, minced
1 teaspoon kosher salt
2 tablespoons tomato paste
2 cups heavy cream
½ cup freshly grated Parmesan cheese, plus extra for garnish
1 pound fettuccine pasta, cooked according to package directions
½ cup minced fresh basil

In a medium skillet over medium heat, add butter. Once butter is melted, add the shallots, garlic and salt. Saute until shallots are softened, about 5 minutes. Stir in tomato paste and saute until the shallots take on the tomato paste's red color, about 2 minutes. Stir in heavy cream and Parmesan cheese. Simmer for 8 to 10 minutes, until the tomato cream sauce has thickened. Pour sauce over pasta and toss until pasta is well coated. Transfer to a serving dish and garnish with Parmesan cheese and fresh basil.

Sausage & Bacon Lasagna

Lasagna is one beautiful, comforting mess. This one especially is, with pasta, lots of sausage, bacon and three kinds of cheese. I often make this on Saturday night or Sunday morning and keep it in the fridge until Sunday dinner time. Lasagna makes for the most kick-backed Sunday dinner. Maybe a good movie and the cushy couch would be in order?

Yields 8 servings

5 mild Italian sausage links, casings removed
5 strips bacon, diced
½ yellow onion, diced
2 garlic cloves, minced
½ teaspoon kosher salt
½ teaspoon ground pepper
1 tablespoon tomato paste
1 15-ounce can diced tomatoes
2 15-ounce cans tomato sauce

1/2 cup water
2 teaspoons dried basil
1 teaspoon dried oregano
1 teaspoon dried thyme
4 cups shredded mozzarella
1 cup shredded parmesan cheese
12 slices provolone cheese
1 9-ounce box no-boil lasagna sheets
¼ cup chopped fresh basil

In a large skillet over medium-high heat, add sausage, bacon, onion, garlic, salt and pepper.

Saute, breaking up the sausage, until sausage and bacon are cooked through and onion is softened, about 15 minutes. Add tomato paste and saute until the paste is broken up and the onions take on the red color. Pour in the diced tomatoes, tomato sauce and water. Stir in the basil, oregano and thyme. Turn heat to medium-low and simmer for 10 minutes.

Preheat oven to 375 degrees F. In a 9x13 inch pan, ladle in ⅓ of the tomato sauce, covering the bottom of the pan completely. Layer ⅓ of the lasagna sheets over the sauce, being sure to cover all the sauce and allowing for overlapping if needed. Sprinkle on ⅓ of mozzarella and parmesan. Lastly, lay four slices of provolone on top. Repeat and end with cheese on top. Cover pan with foil and bake for 45 minutes. Uncover and bake for an additional 10 minutes, until cheese is completely melted. Let lasagna rest for 10 minutes to allow cheese to set. Garnish with fresh basil over the top.

Sausage and Bacon Lasagna
Toasted Garlic Bread, Pg. 198

Penne with White Beans & Arugula Pesto
Frozen Lemonade, pg. 247

Penne with White Beans & Arugula Pesto

My friend Jess is a bit of a genius when it comes to feeding her two boys. She is always looking for ways to get them excited about eating healthy. One way is giving food a whole new name that they can relate to. So in keeping with her smarty pants ways, I call this pasta "Hulk Pasta." My boys latch right onto that. This pasta is bright green and delicious. Arugula takes the place of the usual basil in this pesto. It's more mild than basil and inexpensive. There are also walnuts instead of pine nuts, another way to cut down on cost.

Yields 6 servings

½ cup walnuts
1 5-ounce box arugula
1 lemon, zested and juiced
2 garlic cloves
½ teaspoon kosher salt
½-¾ cup olive oil
½ cup shredded Parmesan cheese
1 pound penne pasta, prepared according to package directions
1 15-ounce can cannellini beans, drained and rinsed

In a medium saucepan over medium heat, add walnuts. Toast walnuts, stirring occasionally, until they are fragrant and lightly browned, about 5-7 minutes. Pour walnuts into the bowl of a food processor. Add arugula, 2 teaspoons lemon juice, garlic and salt. Process until well combined. With the machine running, add olive oil until desired consistency is achieved. Transfer pesto to a medium bowl and stir in lemon zest and Parmesan. Toss pesto with cooked pasta and cannellini beans.

Soups

Creamy Chicken and Rice Soup 137

Chicken Noodle Soup 138

Slow Cooker Italian Sausage and Vegetable Soup 141

Braised Beef Stew 142

Red Curry Carrot Soup 145

Chorizo Chili 146

Vegetable Orzo Soup 149

Corn Chowder with Bacon and Chives 150

Creamy Chicken and Rice Soup

Back in my food blogging days, a reader asked if I would put together a recipe for a creamy chicken and rice soup that doesn't have any of that cream of chicken soup, creepily slippy-sliding out of a can. Done! Over time, I have tweaked this recipe to its current, perfect state. Truly, this might be my greatest recipe creation ever. I have even made it for 100 people for one of my husband's catered events. It is savory, hearty and soothing, a soup everyone is happy to come home to.

Yields 6 servings

½ cup long grain white rice, prepared according to package directions

2 tablespoons extra virgin olive oil
1 yellow onion, diced
1 carrot, peeled and diced
2 celery stalks, diced
2 garlic cloves, minced
1 teaspoon kosher salt
½ teaspoon ground pepper

1 teaspoon dried thyme
½ teaspoon dried sage
8 cups low-sodium chicken stock
2 boneless, skinless chicken breasts
¾ cup heavy cream
2 tablespoons butter, softened
2 tablespoons all-purpose flour
2 tablespoons chopped fresh flat-leaf parsley

Prepare rice and set aside.

In a large pot over medium heat, add olive oil. Once oil is heated, add onion, carrot, celery, garlic, salt and pepper. Saute until vegetables are softened, about 10 minutes. Add thyme and sage and stir until combined. Turn heat to high and pour in chicken stock. Bring to a boil. Add chicken breasts, cover the pot and simmer until chicken is cooked through, about 20 minutes.

Remove chicken from the soup and reduce heat to medium-low and cover the pot. Let the chicken sit until cool enough to handle. Shred the chicken into small, bite-sized pieces. Uncover and add back into the soup. Add the prepared rice and heavy cream. Stir until combined and increase heat to medium-high.

In a small bowl, combine softened butter and flour. Stir it into a paste with a rubber scraper. Stir butter flour mixture into the soup until well combined and the soup is thickened. Simmer for an additional 10 minutes, stirring often. Stir in chopped fresh parsley.

Chicken Noodle Soup

You know, I could have written this recipe to call for homemade stock and homemade egg noodles, but chances are, when you or a loved one have a cold, the last thing on your mind is rolling out egg noodles or boiling a whole chicken to extract every ounce of flavor. Instead, this recipe is designed for people with runny noses and tired eyes who are in need of easy, comforting sustenance. Just get that chicken stock boiling and dump everything in. Hopefully this gets you well on your way to happiness and health.

Yields 6 servings

12 cups low-sodium chicken stock
1 carrot, peeled and diced
2 celery stalks, diced
1 yellow onion, diced
1 teaspoon dried thyme
½ teaspoon kosher salt
¼ teaspoon ground pepper
2 boneless, skinless chicken breasts
8 ounces egg noodles
¼ cup chopped fresh flat-leaf parsley
⅛ teaspoon hot sauce, like Tabasco

In a large pot over high heat, add chicken stock, carrots, celery, onion, thyme, salt and pepper. Bring to a boil and add chicken breasts. Cover pot and boil on high for 20 minutes, or until the chicken's internal temperature reaches 165 degrees F. Remove chicken from the soup and set aside to cool. Add egg noodles and stir well. Boil for 10 minutes. Once the chicken is cool enough to handle, shred into bite-sized pieces. Stir shredded chicken back into the soup. Stir in parsley and hot sauce.

Slow-Cooker Italian Sausage & Vegetable Soup

This soup has three things going for it: sausage, slow cooker and loads of healthful veggies and beans. Everyone loves a good slow cooker recipe, something to throw together in the morning and let simmer throughout the day. This recipe involves a bit more than just throw-in-the-pot-and-stir. To avoid the inevitable evening dinner time chaos, take a few moments in the morning to chop up the zucchini and kale and also cook up those Italian sausages, so they will be ready to stir in before serving time. On your way home, drop by your local bakery and pick up a loaf of good, crusty bread.

Yields 8 servings

2 15-ounce cans diced tomatoes

1 15-ounce can tomato sauce

1 15-ounce can cannellini beans, drained and rinsed

1 15-ounce can kidney beans, drained and rinsed

3 cups low-sodium chicken stock

1 yellow onion, diced

2 garlic cloves, minced

1 teaspoon kosher salt

1 teaspoon dried basil

1/2 teaspoon dried oregano

1/2 teaspoon dried rosemary

1/2 teaspoon dried thyme

⅛ teaspoon fennel seed

⅛ teaspoon crushed red pepper flakes

1-1 ½ pounds sweet Italian sausage links

1 small zucchini, quartered lengthwise and sliced

2 kale leaves, stemmed and roughly chopped

Shredded Parmesan cheese, for serving

In the slow cooker pot, add diced tomatoes, tomato sauce, both beans, chicken stock, onion, garlic, salt, basil, oregano, rosemary, thyme, fennel and red pepper flakes. Stir well to combine and set slow cooker to low. Cook for 6 hours.

In a large skillet over medium heat, cook sausage links for 15 minutes, flipping once, until sausage is cooked through and set aside. Once cool enough to handle, slice sausage into ½-inch thick slices. Add sausage, zucchini and kale to the slow cooker and stir well to combine. Cook on high for 30 minutes. Serve soup with Parmesan cheese on top.

Braised Beef Stew

My heart begins to beat faster when I think about this beef stew. Chunks of beef are braised for 2 hours in a savory broth and become tender and juicy. That same beef broth gets soaked into fresh vegetables, making them irresistible. The only thing missing is a big, fat dinner roll as a bowl cleaner-upper. This soup will change how you think of beef stew.

Yields 6 servings

2-2½ pounds beef chuck roast, cut into 1 inch pieces

2 tablespoons all-purpose flour

1 teaspoon kosher salt

½ teaspoon ground pepper

4 tablespoons extra virgin olive oil, divided

1 yellow onion, halved and quartered

1 tablespoon chopped fresh rosemary

3 garlic cloves, minced

8 cups beef stock

2 bay leaves

3 russet potatoes, chopped

4 carrots, peeled and sliced

½ cup frozen green peas

2 tablespoons chopped fresh parsley

Preheat oven to 350 degrees F.

In a large bowl, add the meat and sprinkle the flour, salt and pepper on top. Toss to combine.

In a large, oven-proof pot over medium-high heat, add 2 tablespoons of olive oil. Once oil is heated, add a few chunks of meat. Brown and turn, about 1-2 minutes per side. Once browned, transfer to a bowl. Repeat with remaining meat. If the pan gets dry, add a few tablespoons of olive oil before the next batch.

After all meat is browned, reduce heat to medium and add two remaining tablespoons of olive oil, onion and rosemary, being sure to scrape up the browned bits of meat on the bottom of the pan. Cook until onions are softened, about 5 minutes.

Add garlic and saute for 1 additional minute. Turn heat to high and pour in the beef stock and add the bay leaves. Add the meat back into the pot, being sure all meat is covered in stock. Allow to come to a boil. Once boiling, cover and put the pot into the oven and let braise for 2 hours.

After 2 hours, take the stew out of the oven and set on the stove top. Set heat to medium-high. Stir in the potatoes and carrots. Simmer for 20-30 minutes, or until the vegetables are tender. Stir in the frozen peas and chopped parsley.

Red Curry Carrot Soup

Besides this soup warming up your tummy, its slight spice will also warm up your tastebuds. Sharp, fragrant ginger pairs with the sweetness of the carrots and coconut milk, and just like it always does, bright, fresh cilantro brings all those flavors full circle. I would like to imagine that a thermos of this soup would be superb after a run down the ski slopes or the shaping of a snowman. Oh wait, don't forget some pita bread for dipping!

Yields 6 servings

2 tablespoons extra virgin olive oil
1 yellow onion, diced
1 teaspoon kosher salt
1 tablespoon grated fresh ginger
1 garlic clove, minced
5 cups peeled and chopped carrots
5 cups vegetable stock
1 14-ounce can coconut milk
1 tablespoon red curry paste
2 tablespoons chopped fresh cilantro, for garnish

In a large pot over medium heat, add olive oil. Once oil is heated, add onion and salt. Saute until the onion is softened, about 10 minutes. Add ginger and garlic and saute for 1 additional minute. Add carrots and stir well. Turn heat to high and pour in vegetable stock. Cover and boil until carrots are tender, about 15 minutes. Once carrots are tender, remove pot from the heat and blend soup in batches in a blender until smooth and pour back into the pot or use an immersion blender. Put the pot back on the heat. Turn heat to medium. Whisk in coconut milk and red curry paste.

Serve soup with a little cilantro sprinkled on top.

Chorizo Chili

Years ago, while living in Rancho Cucamonga, CA, my neighbor and I took on the church chili cook-off. We were determined to win the dang thing. My neighbor brought over a recipe she was sure would win. Its secret ingredient was chorizo. We made the recipe, won the cook-off, and I walked away with some fancy new dollar store hot pads. I never forgot how great the chorizo tasted in it, so a few years later, I came up with my own recipe, using chorizo. The chorizo gives it a little extra oomph with a spicy, meaty kick. If you are concerned about the heat, just eliminate the chile powder as a precaution.

Yields 6 servings

2 tablespoons extra virgin olive oil

1 yellow onion, diced

1 green bell pepper, diced

4 garlic cloves, minced

1 teaspoon kosher salt

1½ pounds ground beef

4 links fresh chorizo sausage, casings removed

1 15-ounce can diced tomatoes

1 15-ounce can tomato sauce

1 15-ounce can kidney beans, drained and rinsed

1 15-ounce can black beans, drained and rinsed

1½ cups water

1 tablespoon unsweetened cocoa powder

2 teaspoons ground cumin

2 teaspoons dried oregano

½ teaspoon chile powder

Sour cream and shredded cheese, for serving

In a large pot over medium-high heat, add olive oil. Once oil is heated, add onion, green bell pepper, garlic, salt and ground beef. Saute, until the vegetables are softened and the ground beef is cooked through, about 15 minutes. Transfer ground beef mixture to a plate lined with a paper towel to drain. Add the chorizo to the pot and saute, while breaking up the chorizo. Once the chorizo is cooked through, about 5 minutes, add the ground beef mixture back into the pot. Stir in diced tomatoes, tomato sauce, kidney beans, black beans, water, cocoa powder, cumin, oregano and chile powder. Stir well and reduce heat to medium-low. Simmer, partially covered, for 30 minutes, stirring occasionally. Serve with sour cream and shredded cheese on top.

Vegetable Orzo Soup

Here is a good ol' hearty vegetable soup. All you need is carrots, celery, onions, tomatoes and potatoes combine with orzo pasta for a substantial soup without the need for meat. Secret to this fantastic vegetable soup? Just a bit of Worcestershire. Trust me, it takes the soup to the next level.

Yields 6 servings

2 tablespoons extra virgin olive oil
2 carrots, peeled and diced
2 celery ribs, diced
1 yellow onion, diced
2 garlic cloves, minced
1½ teaspoons kosher salt
1 teaspoon dried thyme

½ teaspoon ground pepper
8 cups vegetable stock
1 15-ounce can diced tomatoes
1 russet potato, peeled and diced
½ cup orzo pasta
¾ teaspoon worcestershire sauce

In a large pot over medium heat, add olive oil. Once oil is heated, add carrots, celery, onion, garlic, salt, thyme and pepper. Saute until vegetables are softened, about 10 minutes. Turn heat up to high and add vegetable stock and diced tomatoes. Bring to a boil. Once boiling, add diced potato. Boil for 10 minutes, stirring occasionally, until potatoes are tender. Stir in orzo and boil for an additional 15 minutes, until orzo is tender and cooked through. Stir in worcestershire sauce.

Corn Chowder with Bacon & Chives

This is always the first soup I make when summer starts to cool off and stops being so relentlessly hot, right when corn is at its best. As with most things, fresh is best, but if you don't have fresh corn, go ahead and use frozen. No big deal. Bacon and corn make for a perfect marriage. Bacon is smoky and salty, and the corn is sweet. When these two combine, it's one perfect soup, a perfect soup to wave summer off on its merry way.

Yields 6 servings

5 strips bacon, diced
1 yellow onion, diced
1 teaspoon kosher salt
½ teaspoon ground pepper
2 garlic cloves, minced
¼ cup all-purpose flour
6 cups low-sodium chicken stock
2 cups peeled and diced russet potatoes
2 cups fresh or frozen corn kernels
2 cups heavy cream
2 tablespoons minced fresh chives

In a large pot over medium high heat, add bacon. Saute until bacon is cooked through and crisp. Remove bacon with a slotted spoon and set aside in a small bowl, leaving the bacon fat in the pan. Reduce heat to medium and add onion, salt and pepper. Saute until onion is softened, about 5 minutes. Add garlic and flour and saute until flour is well distributed and lightly browned, about 3 minutes. Increase heat to high and pour in chicken stock. Bring to a boil and stir in potatoes. Boil, stirring occasionally, until potatoes are softened, about 5 minutes. Reduce heat to medium and stir in corn and heavy cream. Simmer for 10 minutes. Stir in chives and cooked bacon.

Corn Chowder with Bacon & Chives
My Mama's Dinner Rolls, pg. 193

Salads & Dressings

Orzo Shrimp with Creamy Dijon Dressing 155

Thai Chicken Salad with Peanut Dressing 156

Rotini Pasta Salad with Summer Vegetables & Red Wine 159

Spring Quinoa Salad with Herb Vinaigrette 160

Chicken & Tortellini Salad with Pesto Vinaigrette 161

Summer Fruit Salad with Honey Lime Dressing 162

Cucumber Tomato Salad with Lemon & Dill 163

Sweet Balsalmic Vinaigrette 164

Apple Cider Vinaigrette 165

Creamy Parmesan Dressing 165

Honey Chipotle Dressing 165

Orzo Shrimp Salad with Creamy Dijon Dressing

This is a salad that always disappears fast when I take it to a barbecue or potluck. Besides this salad being full of color, it also has shrimp, and shrimp is just irresistible. This shrimp salad is tossed in a light dijon dressing that doesn't overpower the shrimp's flavor. Besides a fork being a great vehicle for this, put it in some lettuce cups or a tortilla wrap.

Yields 6 servings

3 pounds cooked medium shrimp, tails removed
1 cup orzo pasta, prepared according to package directions
2 celery stalks, diced
½ green bell pepper, diced
¼ red onion, diced
2 tablespoons fresh flat-leaf parsley, minced
¼ cup extra virgin olive oil
5 tablespoons red wine vinegar
1 tablespoon dijon mustard
1 tablespoon mayonnaise
1 teaspoon kosher salt
1 teaspoon ground pepper

In a large bowl, combine shrimp, orzo, celery, green bell pepper, red onion and parsley. Mix to combine. In a jar with a tight-fitting lid, add olive oil, red wine vinegar, dijon, mayonnaise, salt and pepper. Seal tightly and shake until well combined. Pour dressing over the shrimp mixture and gently toss to combine, being sure shrimp are coated in the dressing. Serve immediately or refrigerate and serve chilled.

Thai Chicken Salad with Peanut Dressing

Chick food. This is chick food. This is what women nibble on at baby showers between oohs and aahs over baby booties. This is what ladies lunch on while the bride-to-be unwraps adorable lingerie and toasters. It is the perfect salad for such events. It's hearty enough to be a meal because of the variety of vegetables and shredded chicken. Then it's dressed with a sweet, peanutty dressing that appeals to just about anyone.

Yields 6 servings

For the chicken:

2 boneless, skinless chicken breasts

Extra virgin olive oil, for seasoning

Kosher salt and ground pepper, for seasoning

For the salad:

1 head romaine lettuce, chopped

⅓ cup chopped fresh cilantro

1 red bell pepper, thinly sliced

½ cup frozen shelled edamame, thawed

½ seedless cucumber, chopped

½ cup chopped peanuts

For the dressing:

¼ cup smooth peanut butter

2 tablespoons granulated sugar

2 tablespoons vegetable oil

2 tablespoons honey

2 tablespoons rice vinegar

1 tablespoon soy sauce

1½ teaspoons kosher salt

¼ teaspoon cayenne pepper

Preheat oven to 400 degrees F. Set chicken breasts on a baking sheet. Rub a small amount of olive oil onto each one and season each with salt and pepper. Roast for 25-30 minutes, or until an inserted thermometer reaches 165 degrees F. Allow to cool, shred into bite-sized pieces and set aside.

In a small bowl, combine peanut butter, sugar, vegetable oil, honey, rice vinegar, soy sauce, remaining 1½ teaspoons salt and cayenne pepper. Whisk well and set aside.

In a large bowl, combine romaine lettuce, cilantro, red bell pepper, edamame, cucumber and peanuts. Add chicken and toss until well combined. Drizzle peanut dressing evenly over the top. Toss well. Serve immediately.

Rotini Pasta Salad with Summer Vegetables
& Red Wine Vinaigrette

Spring Quinoa Salad with Herb Vinaigrette, Pg. 160

Chicken & Tortellini Salad with Pesto Vinaigrette, Pg.161

Summer Fruit Salad with Honey Lime Dressing, Pg. 162

Rotini Pasta Salad with Summer Vegetables & Red Wine Vinaigrette

Here is what you are going to bring to that neighborhood barbecue, office potluck or family dinner. Who doesn't love a big scoop of pasta salad dressed with a perfectly tangy dressing and loaded with fresh, crunchy vegetables? In the summertime, I like to make a batch of this and keep it in the fridge so my hungry hippos (aka children) can have a quick lunch or dinner when we are too busy having fun to stop and cook.

Yields 8 servings

1 pound rotini pasta, cooked according to package directions
1 seedless cucumber, quartered lengthwise and chopped
1 red bell pepper, diced
1 bunch green onions, diced
8 ounces grape tomatoes, halved
1 15-ounce can black olives, drained
½ cup red wine vinegar
3 tablespoons fresh lemon juice
1 tablespoon honey
1½ teaspoons kosher salt
½ teaspoon ground pepper
¾ cup extra virgin olive oil
¼ cup fresh flat-leaf parsley, chopped
1 4-ounce package crumbled feta cheese

Cook pasta, drain and rinse under cold water to cool. Drain very well and pour pasta into a large bowl. Stir in cucumbers, red bell peppers, green onions, grape tomatoes and black olives. Set aside.

In a medium bowl, combine red wine vinegar, lemon juice, honey, salt and pepper. Whisk well. While whisking, slowly pour in olive oil. Whisk in parsley. Pour vinaigrette over pasta and vegetables. Stir well. Fold in feta cheese. Serve immediately or refrigerate and serve chilled.

Spring Quinoa Salad with Herb Vinaigrette

Why is this titled Spring Quinoa Salad? Because here is when you get a chance to use those tiny, tender spring vegetables in your garden. The ones who have poked their little heads up first and said, "Pick me! Pick me!" Don't worry little veggies; it's your turn. Green peas, radishes and green onions combine with quinoa for a light, healthful salad fit for a luncheon, dinner get-together or plain old midnight snack that won't undo your day.

Yields 6 servings

2½ cups water
1 teaspoon kosher salt
1 cup quinoa, rinsed well
1 15-ounce can cannellini beans, drained and rinsed
¾ cup green peas, fresh or frozen
¾ cup thinly sliced radishes
⅓ cup thinly sliced green onion

½ teaspoon kosher salt
¼ teaspoon ground pepper
1 tablespoon minced fresh oregano
1 tablespoon minced fresh sage
1 tablespoon minced fresh thyme
3 tablespoons white wine vinegar
¼ cup extra virgin olive oil

In a large saucepan over high heat, add water and 1 teaspoon salt. Once boiling, add quinoa and cannellini beans. Boil, uncovered, until most of the liquid is absorbed and the quinoa is sputtering, about 10-12 minutes. Turn heat to low, add green peas and simmer until all liquid is evaporated, about 5-7 minutes. Remove from heat and scoop quinoa and beans into a bowl. Set aside and allow to cool completely.

Stir radishes and green onions into the quinoa mixture, breaking up the chunks of compacted quinoa. In a small bowl, combine ½ teaspoon salt, pepper, oregano, sage, thyme and vinegar. Slowly whisk in olive oil. Pour vinaigrette over the quinoa, beans and vegetables. Serve immediately, or refrigerate and serve chilled.

Pictured on Page 158.

Chicken & Tortellini Salad with Pesto Vinaigrette

This is also called "Road Trip Salad." Make it the night before you leave, pack it into reusable containers and tape a fork to the side. Once you are in the car, restless as can be and sick of Abba Zabbas and Charleston Chews, pull this salad out of the ice chest and wow the crowd. The hearty chunks of chicken breast, fresh veggies and tortellini dressed in a pesto vinaigrette are sure to banish the road trip blues.

Yields 6 servings

2 boneless, skinless chicken breasts
Extra virgin olive oil, for seasoning
Kosher salt and ground pepper, for seasoning
1 9-ounce package fresh cheese tortellini
1 10-ounce carton cherry tomatoes, quartered

2 cups baby spinach
¼ red onion, thinly sliced
½ cup prepared pesto
2 teaspoons red wine vinegar
⅓ cup extra virgin olive oil

Preheat oven to 400 degrees F. Set chicken breasts on a baking sheet. Rub a small amount of olive oil onto each one and season each with salt and pepper. Roast for 25-30 minutes, or until an inserted thermometer reaches 165 degrees F. Allow to cool, shred into bite-sized pieces and set aside.

In a large pot of boiling salted water, cook tortellini according to package directions. Drain and set aside to cool. In a small bowl, combine pesto and red wine vinegar. While whisking, slowly drizzle in olive oil.

In a large bowl combine, chicken, tortellini, tomatoes, spinach and red onion. Drizzle pesto vinaigrette over the top and toss well. Serve immediately or refrigerate and serve chilled.

Pictured on Page 158.

Summer Fruit Salad with Honey Lime Dressing

Here is how you enhance what doesn't need enhancing. This makes summer flavors more intense than they need to be. Sweet, plump, juicy fruit covered in a tart dressing makes this dish almost like dessert. Speaking of which, this fruit salad would be dreamy over some pineapple sorbet.

Yields 6 servings

2 limes, zested and juiced
¼ cup honey
¼ teaspoon pure vanilla extract
⅛ teaspoon kosher salt
6 cups cubed watermelon
3 nectarines, pitted and cut into chunks
1 pound strawberries, hulled and quartered

In a small bowl, combine 2 tablespoons lime juice, lime zest, honey, vanilla extract and salt. Whisk well to combine and set aside.

In a large bowl, combine watermelon, nectarines and strawberries. Drizzle dressing over the top and gently stir to coat fruit in dressing. Serve immediately.

Here are a few recipes to help you enjoy the satisfaction of homemade dressing. All are simple to make and will last in the fridge for a couple weeks. With the vinaigrettes, you can use them as a marinade for steaks, shrimp or chicken. If you do that, let the meat sit in the marinade for at least 6 hours. Also, I would double the recipe if you are marinating, just to be sure your lunch or dinner gets a proper dunk before grilling.

Pictured on Page 158.

Cucumber Tomato Salad with Lemon & Dill

This salad pays homage to my childhood. My mom was a born and bred Northern California girl. Her father, a WWII paratrooper, was a master gardener. He knew his way around tomato plants and eggplant vines. My dad called my grandpa's cantaloupes "Erv-loupes" because no one could grow a cantaloupe like Grandpa Erv. Because of his proficient green thumb, my mom grew up eating fresh vegetables of every kind. When she had her own children, she made it a point to feed us a wide variety of fresh veggies. This cucumber and tomato salad is just like the one she would set on our dinner table almost weekly. Crunchy cucumbers and tangy tomatoes, dressed with lemon and dill, evoke the essence of summer.

Yields 6 servings

1 seedless cucumber, quartered lengthwise and chopped
1 8-ounce carton cherry tomatoes, quartered
2 tablespoons chopped fresh dill
1 lemon, zested and juiced
1 tablespoon capers
1 tablespoon extra virgin olive oil
½ teaspoon kosher salt
¼ teaspoon ground pepper

In a large bowl, combine cucumber, tomatoes, dill, lemon zest, 1 teaspoon lemon juice, capers, olive oil, salt and pepper. Gently stir to combine. Serve immediately or refrigerate and serve chilled.

Pictured on Page 13.

Here are a few recipes to help you enjoy the satisfaction of homemade dressing. All are simple to make and will last in the fridge for a couple weeks. With the vinaigrettes, you can use them as a marinade for steaks, shrimp or chicken. If you do that, let the meat sit in the marinade for at least 6 hours. Also, I would double the recipe if you are marinating, just to be sure your lunch or dinner gets a proper dunk before grilling.

Sweet Balsamic Vinaigrette

Yields ¾ cup dressing

½ cup extra virgin olive oil
¼ cup balsamic vinegar
2 garlic cloves, minced

2 tablespoons granulated sugar
½ teaspoon kosher salt
½ teaspoon ground pepper

Add all ingredients to a jar, seal tightly with a lid and shake until well combined.
Serve over green salad or use as a marinade.

Apple Cider Vinaigrette

Yields ¾ cup dressing

½ cup extra virgin olive oil
¼ cup apple cider vinegar
1 tablespoon granulated sugar
1 tablespoon balsamic vinegar

1 teaspoon worcestershire sauce
½ teaspoon kosher salt
½ teaspoon ground pepper

Add all ingredients to a jar, seal tightly with a lid and shake until well combined. Serve over green salad or use as a marinade.

Creamy Parmesan Dressing

Yields 1¼ cup dressing

¾ cup freshly grated Parmesan cheese
½ cup mayonnaise
¼ cup sour cream
2 garlic cloves, minced
1 tablespoon fresh lemon juice

1 tablespoon milk
1 teaspoon worcestershire sauce
½ teaspoon kosher salt
¼ teaspoon ground pepper

Add all ingredients to a medium bowl. Whisk well to combine. Serve over green salad.

Honey Chipotle Dressing

Yields 1⅓ cups dressing

½ cup red wine vinegar
⅓ cup honey
2 teaspoons dijon mustard
1 chipotle pepper, sliced open and seeds removed

½ teaspoon adobo sauce from the chipotle can
½ teaspoon kosher salt
¼ teaspoon dried oregano
1 garlic clove
½ cup extra virgin olive oil

In a blender, combine vinegar, honey, mustard, chipotle pepper, adobo sauce, salt, oregano and garlic. Blend until the garlic and chipotle pepper are well combined. With the blender running, drizzle in the olive oil. Serve over green salad or use as a marinade.

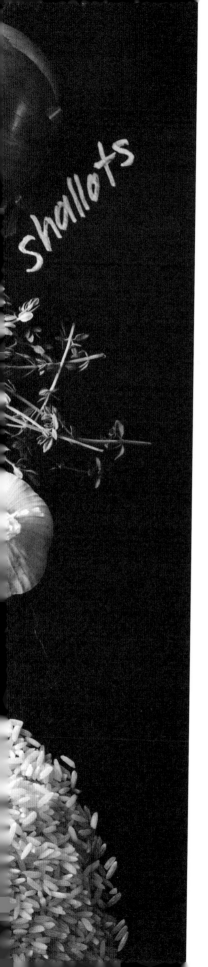

Sides

Roasted Red Potatoes with Rosemary 168

Braised Kale 169

Roasted Cauliflower with Sun-dried Tomato Butter 171

Roasted Garlic Mashed Potatoes 172

Baked Artichokes with Lemon-Garlic Mayo 175

Roasted Brussel Sprouts with Browned Butter 176

Guacamole 178

Walnut Green Beans 179

Pine Nut & Herb Rice Pilaf 181

Baked Beans 182

Sauteed Corn with Lime & Queso Fresco 184

Potato Pancakes 185

Bulgur Pilaf with Red Peppers & Almonds 186

Refried Beans 187

Mexican Rice 188

Toasted Couscous with Leaks & Garlic 189

Roasted Red Potatoes with Rosemary

I almost feel stupid for writing a recipe for something so simple. But I suppose every cook should have a method for roasted potatoes. Roasted potatoes are one of the simplest, cheapest and most delicious side dishes. No red potatoes? Feel free to use whatever potatoes you have on hand. This method of roasting can be applied to nearly any vegetable. Ever tried roasted broccoli? Life-changing.

Yields 6 servings

2½ pounds red potatoes, chopped
2½ tablespoons extra virgin olive oil
1 teaspoon kosher salt
½ teaspoon ground pepper
1 tablespoon fresh rosemary, chopped

Preheat oven to 425 degrees F. Spray a baking sheet with non-stick spray. Add potatoes, olive oil, salt, pepper and rosemary. Toss well, coating potatoes with oil and spread into a single layer. Roast potatoes for 20-25 minutes, until potatoes are lightly browned and tender in the middle. Serve immediately.

Pictured on Page 66.

Braised Kale

I love it when I can trick my children into eating something so unbelievably good for them. I didn't have to hide it in brownies or macaroni and cheese; I just give it to them straight up and they still eat it! Joke's on them! This kale is that very thing. Try this on your children and laugh maniacally as I do.

Yields 4 servings

2 tablespoons extra virgin olive oil
1 red onion, halved and thinly sliced
1 teaspoon kosher salt
½ teaspoon ground pepper
1 garlic clove, minced
7 packed cups stemmed and roughly chopped kale
2 cups low-sodium chicken stock
Splash of red wine vinegar

In a large skillet over medium heat, add olive oil. Once oil is heated, add onions, salt and pepper. Saute until the onions are softened, about 10 minutes. Add garlic and saute for 1 additional minute. Stir in kale, tossing gently to combine with the onions and garlic. Pour in chicken stock and turn heat to high. Partially cover pan, stirring occasionally. Simmer for 10 minutes, or until liquid evaporates. Add vinegar and toss well. Cook for 1 minute. Pour kale onto a serving platter.

Pictured on Page 62.

Roasted Cauliflower with Sun-dried Tomato Butter

It is an absolute tragedy that there are some people on this earth that have never had roasted cauliflower. They only know it in its steamed or boiled form. No salty sweet, caramelized cauliflower. Only mushy, bland cauliflower. To gild the lily, this cauliflower is also topped with a tangy, garlicky butter. Not only does it make cauliflower irresistible, it also makes it beautiful. Specks of bright red tomato and bright green chives throughout. It might be the prettiest cauliflower to ever sit at your dinner table.

Yields 6 servings

¼ cup unsalted butter, softened
2 tablespoons freshly grated Parmesan cheese
3 oil-packed sun-dried tomato halves, patted dry of excess oil and minced
1 teaspoon minced fresh chives
1 garlic clove, minced
1 head cauliflower, trimmed into bite-sized florets
2½ tablespoons extra virgin olive oil
1 teaspoon kosher salt
½ teaspoon ground pepper

Preheat oven to 425 degrees F.

In a small bowl, combine butter, Parmesan cheese, sun-dried tomatoes, chives and garlic. With a rubber scraper, mix until well combined. Set aside.

Spray a baking sheet with non-stick spray. Add cauliflower, olive oil, salt and pepper. Toss well, coating cauliflower with oil and spread into a single layer. Roast for 20-25 minutes, until cauliflower is lightly browned and tender in the middle.

Transfer roasted cauliflower to a large bowl and add sun-dried tomato butter. Gently toss until butter is melted and well-combined. Transfer to a serving bowl.

Roasted Garlic Mashed Potatoes

Me and potatoes, best friends: fried, boiled, roasted, stuffed, mashed, grilled. Anyway you give me a potato, I will quickly and happily consume it. This recipe is always my favorite way to eat a tater. It takes a perfect mashed potato and gives it a new flare with bits of roasted, sweet garlic mixed in. No need for gravy.

Yields 6 servings

1 garlic bulb
3 tablespoons extra virgin olive oil
6 russet potatoes, peeled and chopped
⅓ cup half and half
⅓ cup unsalted butter
2 teaspoons kosher salt
1 teaspoon ground pepper

Preheat oven to 300 degrees F. Cut off the top of the garlic bulb, exposing the garlic cloves, and set onto two sheets of aluminum foil. Pour olive oil over the top of the garlic bulb. Wrap the foil loosely around the bulb and place on the oven rack. Roast for 2 hours, until garlic cloves are golden. Remove from oven and set aside to cool. Once cooled, squeeze garlic cloves out of the the garlic bulb, discarding the garlic skins and bulb. Set roasted garlic cloves on a cutting board and with the flat edge of the knife, scrape the garlic cloves over the board, making a paste. Scrape roasted garlic paste into a small bowl and set aside.

Add potatoes to a large pot and cover with water. Set over high heat and bring to a boil. Boil until potatoes are fork tender, about 10 minutes. Drain potatoes and pour into a large mixing bowl. While the potatoes are boiling, add half and half, and butter to a small saucepan over medium heat and melt butter, stirring occasionally. Once melted, remove from heat and set aside.

Mash potatoes with a masher until smooth. Pour half and half mixture over the potatoes and add salt, pepper and roasted garlic paste. Using a rubber spatula, fold the potatoes over themselves, combining all ingredients. Be sure you do not overmix.

Baked Artichokes with Lemon-Garlic Mayo

When you have a well-made artichoke, you might not need anything else in this world. This here is a well-made artichoke. Charred edges, soft petals, excellent dipping sauce. And this is so much less mess than boiling them. I wish my family didn't like these so there would be more left for me.

Yields 6 servings

3 large artichokes
1 lemon, zested and cut in half
1½ teaspoons kosher salt, divided
6 teaspoons extra virgin olive oil, divided
1 cup mayonnaise
2 garlic cloves, minced
1 tablespoon chopped fresh flat-leaf parsley
½ teaspoon worcestershire sauce
Lemon wedges, for serving

Preheat oven to 425 degrees F. Cut six sheets of foil and set aside.

Cut each artichoke in half lengthwise and immediately rub half a lemon over the cut side, while gently squeezing the lemon, spreading the juice over the surface. Sprinkle ¼ teaspoon of salt over the cut side. Pour 1 teaspoon of olive oil on one sheet of foil. Put artichoke cut side down on the oil. Pull up the sides of the foil and wrap the artichoke half. Set on a baking sheet, cut side down. Repeat with the remaining artichoke halves. Bake the artichokes for 1 hour.

While the artichokes are baking, in a small bowl combine mayonnaise, garlic, chopped parsley, worcestershire, 1 teaspoon lemon juice and 2 teaspoons lemon zest. Stir well and set aside.

Once artichokes are baked, remove from foil and set aside until cool enough to touch. Once cooled, with a spoon, scoop out the middle, discarding the choke. Serve artichokes with lemon-garlic mayo and lemon wedges.

Roasted Brussel Sprouts with Browned Butter

Twas the night before Christmas 2010. I had imagined up a lovely dinner for the holiday's eve. Roasted herb chicken, fancy mixed greens with a perfect vinaigrette, silky smooth mashed potatoes, seasonal creme brulee. And then I had to find a use for those pesky brussel sprouts that were forgotten in the back of the fridge, about to turn. I decided to roast them, and as an afterthought, toss them in some browned butter. Well, who would have thought they were the hit of the holiday night! My husband wanted nothing more for Christmas than a repeat of these brussel sprouts on a regular basis. The nuttiness of the butter with the caramelized brussel sprouts is a little bit of paradise on a plate.

Yields 6 servings

½ cup unsalted butter
1 pound brussel sprouts, tough ends trimmed off and cut in half lengthwise
2½ tablespoons extra virgin olive oil
1 teaspoon kosher salt
½ teaspoon ground pepper

In a small saucepan over medium heat, melt butter. Once butter is melted, stir butter occasionally until butter is browned and fragrant, about 10 minutes. Pour butter into a small bowl and set aside.

Preheat oven to 425 degrees F. Spray a baking sheet with non-stick spray. Add brussel sprouts, olive oil, salt and pepper. Toss well, coating brussel sprouts with oil and spread into a single layer. Roast for 20-25 minutes, until brussel sprouts are tender and lightly browned.

Once roasted, transfer brussel sprouts to a large mixing bowl. With a small spoon, spoon the top separated layer of browned butter on top of the brussel sprouts and discard the dark brown butter solids in the bottom of the bowl. Toss the brussel sprouts until they are coated in butter. Pour into a serving dish.

Guacamole

Why can't we just eat guacamole for every meal? I would. Hand me a bowl of guac and some chips and I make embarrassingly light work of it. Creamy avocados with a little spiciness from the garlic and jalapeno and then some smokiness from the cumin. Oh, I can taste it now! Should I let you in on a little catering trick my husband uses? If you are making guac for a big group, use the grocery store deli's pre-made pico de gallo and mix that in instead of you doing all the chopping. Genius, right?

Yields 6 servings

5 avocados
1 lime, halved
1 medium tomato, diced, seeds and membranes removed and discarded
1 jalapeno, seeded and minced
½ cup red onion, diced
¼ cup fresh cilantro, chopped
1 garlic clove, minced
½ teaspoon kosher salt
¼ teaspoon ground cumin
⅛ teaspoon chile powder

Halve the avocados. Remove the pit and using a spoon, scoop the flesh into a medium bowl. Squeeze the lime juice directly over the avocados. Using two small knives, roughly chop the avocados by passing the knives by each other in a crossing motion. Add the tomato, jalapeno, onion, cilantro, garlic, salt, cumin and chile powder. Using a rubber scraper, gently mix all ingredients until well combined. Serve immediately or cover with plastic wrap and refrigerate.

Pictured on Page 106.

Walnut Green Beans

Every night I make dinner; I try to be sure I serve some type of green vegetable on the side. My family likes steamed green beans, but I think I have done them too often. This helps spice things up a bit. Nutty walnut oil and toasted walnuts give green beans a whole new reason to live, or in our case, be eaten. Looking for walnut oil? Look on the top shelf, above the olive and vegetable oils.

Yields 6 servings

½ cup chopped walnuts
2 tablespoons walnut oil
1 pound fresh green beans, ends trimmed off
½ teaspoon kosher salt

In a large skillet over medium heat, add walnuts. Toast walnuts, tossing occasionally, until fragrant and lightly browned, about 10 minutes. Pour walnuts into a small bowl and set aside. Set skillet back on the heat and add the walnut oil, green beans and salt. Saute until beans are lightly browned, about 5 minutes.

Transfer green beans to a serving dish and sprinkle toasted walnuts on top.

Pictured on Page 41.

Pine Nut & Herb Rice Pilaf

Here is a dish that really lets fresh herbs shine. Would you like to know the secret to making people think you are a better cook than you are? Use fresh herbs. Dried herbs just aren't up to snuff. Fresh herbs add more than just their flavor. They add beautiful bright green color and a slight sophistication to your meal. But of course, if you do not have fresh herbs, dried herbs are your next best option. If you are substituting dried herbs for fresh, halve the amount. For example, where this recipe calls for 1 tablespoon of minced fresh rosemary, you can substitute ½ tablespoon of dried rosemary.

Yields 6 servings

⅓ cup pine nuts
2 tablespoons unsalted butter
1 shallot, minced
1 teaspoon kosher salt
½ teaspoon ground pepper
1 garlic clove, minced

1 tablespoon minced fresh rosemary
1 tablespoon minced fresh sage
1 tablespoon minced fresh thyme
1 cup long grain white rice
2 cups low-sodium chicken stock

In a medium saucepan over medium heat, add pine nuts. Toast pine nuts until they are fragrant and lightly browned, about 5 minutes. Pour nuts into a small bowl and set aside. Place the saucepan back on the heat, reduce heat to medium and add butter. Once butter is melted, add shallots, salt and pepper. Saute shallots until softened, about 5 minutes. Add garlic, rosemary, sage and thyme and saute for one additional minute. Pour in rice and stir to combine. Turn heat to high and pour in chicken stock. Bring to a boil. Cover and reduce heat to low. Simmer for 15 minutes. Uncover and stir. Cover and set back on the heat and cook for 10 more minutes.

Once rice is cooked, remove pan from heat and add pine nuts. Stir well and transfer to a serving dish.

Baked Beans

I know you are going to eat at least one hot dog this summer. It's okay, you are among friends; you can admit it. When you do enjoy that hot dog, enjoy a pile of this on the side. Creamy white beans braised in a sweet, tangy barbecue sauce and accented with chunks of bacon. These beans are a summertime essential.

Yields 6 servings

1 yellow onion, diced
5 strips bacon, diced
2 teaspoons kosher salt
½ teaspoon ground pepper
2 cups water
⅔ cup brown sugar
⅔ cup ketchup
2 tablespoons dijon mustard
2 tablespoons molasses
2 teaspoons apple cider vinegar
3 15 ounce cans cannellini beans or navy beans, drained and rinsed

Preheat oven to 400 degrees F.

In a large, oven-proof pot over medium heat, add onion, bacon, salt and pepper. Saute until bacon is browned and onion is softened, about 10 minutes. In a medium bowl, combine water, brown sugar, ketchup, dijon mustard, molasses and vinegar. Whisk well to combine. Pour into the onion and bacon mixture. Add beans and gently stir to combine. Simmer for 5 minutes, stirring occasionally. Put the lid on the pot and put it into the oven for 30 minutes.

Sauteed Corn with Lime & Queso Fresco

While this is great as a side dish, it's also awesome as a salsa with tortilla chips or spooned into tacos. Sweet corn topped with fresh lime juice and zest and queso fresco cheese. Lots of pretty colors and bright flavors.

Yields 6 servings

2 tablespoons unsalted butter
3 cups fresh or frozen corn
1 teaspoon kosher salt
1 lime, zested and juiced
¼ cup crumbled queso fresco

In a large skillet over medium-high heat, add butter. Once butter is melted, add corn and salt. Saute until corn is lightly browned, about 5 minutes. Remove pan from heat and stir in lime zest and juice. Transfer corn to a serving dish and sprinkle queso fresco on top.

Pictured on Page 98.

Potato Pancakes

My favorite way to eat these is with an egg over-easy and a dash of Tabasco. Crisp potatoes, runny yolk and a bit of heat. My 4 year old, taking a tip from his daddy, likes these with a dab of crème fraîche and strips of smoked salmon. But my oldest son keeps it simple: nothing but ketchup. Whatever you put on these, they are sure to be a hit.

Yields 8 pancakes

6 russet potatoes, peeled and quartered lengthwise
2 tablespoons all-purpose flour
1 egg, lightly beaten
1½ teaspoons kosher salt
½ teaspoon ground pepper
¼ cup vegetable oil, divided

Preheat oven to 200 degrees. Set a baking sheet in the oven.

In a food processor fitted with the shredding disc, shred the potatoes. Transfer to a towel, gather the sides up and twist, squeezing out as much moisture as possible.

Add the shredded potatoes to a large mixing bowl. Add flour, egg, salt and pepper. Toss to combine. On another baking sheet, divide potato mixture into eight even piles.

In a large skillet over medium-high heat, add 1 tablespoon vegetable oil. Once oil is heated, add two of the potato piles. Flatten with a spatula. Cook until golden on the edges, about 2 minutes. Flip and cook on the other side until golden. Remove pancakes from the pan and set on baking sheet in the oven to keep warm. Repeat with remaining potato mixture and vegetable oil.

Pictured on Page 58.

Bulgur Pilaf with Red Peppers & Almonds

What a great, healthy alternative to rice! Bulgur, with its horrible-sounding name, is hearty and packed full of fiber. This dish is simmered in chicken stock and flavored with onions, red bell peppers and garlic. It is great as a side dish or on its own. And guess what? This is another recipe that loves being a leftover. Where do you find quick-cooking bulgur? Look for the bags of Bob's Red Mill products; they have a great one.

Yields 6 servings

2 tablespoons unsalted butter
½ yellow onion, diced
½ red bell pepper, diced
2 garlic cloves, minced
1 teaspoon kosher salt
½ teaspoon ground pepper
1½ cups quick-cooking bulgur
2 cups low-sodium chicken stock
3 tablespoons fresh parsley, chopped
⅓ cup sliced almonds

In a medium pot over medium heat, add butter. Once butter is melted, add onion, bell pepper, garlic, salt and pepper. Saute until onion and bell pepper are softened, about 10 minutes. Add bulgur and stir well to combine. Turn heat to high and pour in chicken stock. Once boiling, reduce heat to low, cover and simmer until all liquid is absorbed and bulgur is tender, about 12 minutes. Remove pot from heat and stir in parsley and almonds.

Pictured on Page 49.

Refried Beans

These beans took me forever to figure out. I wanted smooth and super basic. The kind of beans that are the glue that holds a great Mexican meal together. I found that I prefer bacon fat over lard. I found that the beans have to be cooked very thoroughly to aid in a smooth texture. And I also found that starting with dried beans is essential. Hopefully you can take advantage of all my recipe testing. Believe me, my kids ate so many sub-par beans and hated me for it.

Yields 6 servings

2 pounds dried pinto beans
1 onion, halved and then one half diced
2 teaspoons kosher salt
10 pieces bacon, diced
5 garlic cloves, minced
Kosher salt, for seasoning

In a large slow cooker, add beans, the onion half and salt. Fill with water all the way to the top. Set heat to high and cook for 8 hours or overnight, until the beans are very tender and creamy. Set a strainer over a large bowl and strain the beans, reserving all the cooking liquid and discarding the onion.

Set a large pot over medium high heat. Once heated, add bacon. Saute until bacon fat is rendered and the bacon is crisp. With a slotted spoon, remove bacon and discard, leaving the bacon fat in the pan. Reduce heat to medium and add the diced onion and garlic to the bacon fat and saute until softened, about 5 minutes. Remove the pot from the heat and add the drained beans to the pot and 2 cups of the reserved cooking liquid. With a potato masher, mash the beans until smooth. Add more cooking liquid as needed, to achieve desired consistency. Season to taste with salt.

Pictured on Page 73.

Mexican Rice

The perfect Mexican rice is fluffy, has a slight tomato flavor and a sharp garlic flavor. Its best friend is beans, refried beans. They play together well. I actually don't know if I can eat Mexican rice without refried beans. It just isn't the same without them. If you feel the same way I do, you're in luck. We've added a refried beans recipe on page 187.

Yields 6 servings

2 tablespoons unsalted butter
1½ cups long-grain white rice
½ yellow onion, diced
½ teaspoon kosher salt
3 garlic cloves, minced
2½ cups low-sodium chicken stock
½ cup tomato sauce
1 Roma tomato, diced
¼ teaspoon ground cumin

In a large saucepan over medium-high heat, add butter. Once butter is melted, add rice, onion and salt and saute until rice is lightly browned, about 5 minutes. Add garlic and saute for one additional minute. Turn heat to high and add chicken stock, tomato sauce, diced tomatoes and cumin. Bring to a boil. Cover and reduce heat to low. Simmer for 15 minutes. Uncover and stir. Cover and cook for 10 more minutes. Fluff rice with a fork and transfer to a serving bowl.

Pictured on Page 73.

Toasted Couscous with Leeks & Garlic

I have a confession. I never make this recipe. I know, ridiculous. Why would I never make a recipe I put in my own cookbook? Simple answer: I have little children, ages 7, 4 and 2, to be precise. It's my 2 year old that ruins my couscous making. She is quite unladylike when eating couscous. She shovels it into her mouth with little regard for the mess she is making below her highchair. Have you ever had to sweep up couscous? It's nearly impossible. Tiny, moist little grains prefer to stick to a broom. But if you have a dog that likes toddler mealtime messes, you are in luck! You and your pup will enjoy the light nutty flavor of the couscous paired with lots of garlic and leeks. It's a guaranteed hit.

Yields 6 servings

1½ cups couscous
3 tablespoons unsalted butter
1 leek, halved lengthwise and finely chopped
3 garlic cloves, minced
1 teaspoon kosher salt
1¾ cups low-sodium chicken stock

In a medium saucepan over medium-high heat, add couscous. Stir couscous often, until fragrant and lightly browned, about 5 minutes. Pour couscous into a medium bowl and set aside.

Put pan back on the burner and add butter. Once butter is melted, add leeks, garlic and salt. Saute until leeks are lightly browned, about 5 minutes. Pour in chicken stock and bring to a boil. Once boiling, add toasted couscous. Cover and remove pan from the heat. Let sit for 5 minutes. Fluff with a fork and transfer to a serving dish.

Pictured on Page 84.

Bread

Cornbread Muffins 192

My Mama's Dinner Rolls 193

Buttermilk Biscuits 194

Glazed Coconut Bread 197

Toasted Garlic Bread 198

Homemade Croutons 199

Cornbread Muffins

Who says cornbread is only for chili? It isn't, I assure you. Cornbread likes to appear on the breakfast table and be covered in strawberry jam. It loves lunchboxes and road trips. Its favorite thing is Nutella and leftovers can be made into croutons. Sure, butter it up and put it next to a bowl of chili, but don't limit its possibilities!

Yields 12 muffins

1½ cups cornmeal
½ cup all-purpose flour
½ cup granulated sugar
1½ teaspoons baking powder
1 teaspoon salt
½ teaspoon baking soda
2 eggs
1¼ cups milk
¼ cup vegetable oil

Set oven to 375 degrees F.

Spray a 12-cup muffin pan with non-stick spray and set aside.

In a medium bowl, combine cornmeal, flour, sugar, baking powder, salt and baking soda. Whisk to combine and set aside. In another medium bowl, combine eggs, milk and oil and whisk well. Pour egg mixture into the dry ingredients and whisk to combine.

Divide batter between muffin cups. Bake for 18-20 minutes, until muffin tops are lightly browned. Serve warm.

Pictured on Page 147.

My Mama's Dinner Rolls

Recipe by Sue Peterson

My mom, oh my sweet mother. Whole-wheat bread, orange sweet rolls, pizza dough, cinnamon rolls, fried scones; she has them all down pat. And her dinner rolls are soft, pillowy perfection. It sounds so cliche, but these rolls are piled in a basket at every Thanksgiving dinner and Sunday roast beef feast. After those meals, I am often sent home with a zip-top bag full of feathery rolls. And then for breakfast the next morning, I drown them in butter and honey.

Yields 16 rolls

2½ cups all-purpose flour
¼ cup vital wheat gluten
1½ tablespoons Saf Instant yeast, no substitutes
1½ cups hot water, between 120-130 degrees F
⅓ cup vegetable oil
¼ cup honey
2 eggs

2 teaspoons kosher salt
3¼ cup all-purpose flour, plus ¼ cup more (if needed)
2 tablespoons vegetable oil
2 tablespoons unsalted butter, softened

Add flour, gluten, yeast, water, vegetable oil and honey in a mixing bowl fitted with the paddle attachment. Mix until combined. Cover the mixer and bowl with a towel and let sit for 10 minutes, which will allow the yeast to proof and slightly rise.

Once dough is bubbly, add eggs and salt and mix until combined. Remove the paddle attachment and put on the dough hook attachment. With the mixer running on low, add 3¼ cups flour. Once the flour is incorporated, the dough should feel moist and sticky, but not stick to your fingers. If the dough sticks to your fingers, add ¼ cup more flour. Set mixer to low and knead for 5 minutes. Remove the dough from the bowl and off the dough hook. If you tap the dough, it should sound like a melon.

Spray a 10x15-inch baking sheet with non-stick spray. Pour 2 tablespoons vegetable oil onto the counter and spread it around with your hands. With a rolling pin, roll the dough out to a 18x12-inch square. With a knife, cut the dough into quarters, making 4 squares. Cut each square into 4 strips, making 16 strips. Roll up each strip, gently pressing the end down and set on the prepared baking sheet, seam side down. Lay a lightweight towel on top of the rolls and allow them to rise, doubling in size, for 30-45 minutes. Once risen, set oven to 350 degrees F. When oven is heated, bake rolls for 15-20 minutes. If the rolls begin to brown too quickly, set a large sheet of foil over the top of the rolls. Once baked, brush butter on the tops of the hot rolls with a pastry brush.

Pictured on Page 151.

Buttermilk Biscuits

Boy howdy! Biscuits! Biscuits so fluffy and tall! Biscuits begging for butter, honey or jam! These are the biscuits that would make any Southern granny proud. You have a food processor? Congratulations, you are going to love making these even more. Just let the blades do the part of breaking up the butter. And be sure not to overmix once you pour the buttermilk in.

Yields 8 biscuits

3 cups self-rising flour
1 teaspoon baking powder
1 teaspoon baking soda
½ teaspoon kosher salt
¾ cup unsalted butter, diced
1 cup buttermilk

Set oven to 425 degrees F.

In a large bowl, combine flour, baking powder, baking soda and salt. Mix well with your hands. Add diced butter. With your fingers, break up the butter into the flour until the butter resembles small pebbles. Pour in buttermilk and mix with your hands until all flour is moistened. Transfer dough to a lightly floured surface and gently pat the dough into a 1-inch-thick circle. With a biscuit cutter or the rim of a small drinking glass, cut out eight biscuits, reshaping the dough into a circle if needed. Place the biscuits onto a baking sheet, being sure the edges are touching, and bake for 15-18 minutes, or until the biscuits are lightly browned on top.

Glazed Coconut Bread

Growing up, my mom was not a fan of coconut anything. So naturally, I thought it was horrid too. I hated it right along with my mom. I would say I didn't like Almond Joys and coconut sorbet. Then I got married and my husband insisted my mom was wrong. "Coconut is sensational!", he proclaimed. And what do you know, he was right. I mostly make this bread for my husband, who says he would wear coconut extract as cologne. Sorry Mom, coconut is pretty delish.

Yields 1 loaf

For the bread:
1½ cups all-purpose flour
½ teaspoon salt
½ teaspoon baking powder
¼ teaspoon baking soda
1 cup granulated sugar
½ cup vegetable oil
2 eggs
2 teaspoons coconut extract
½ cup coconut milk

For the glaze:
¼ cup shredded coconut
½ cup powdered sugar
2 tablespoons coconut milk
½ teaspoon coconut extract

Set oven to 325 degrees F.

Spray a 9x5-inch bread pan with non-stick spray and set aside.

In a medium bowl, combine flour, salt, baking powder and baking soda. Whisk well to combine and set aside. In a mixing bowl fitted with the paddle attachment, add sugar and vegetable oil. Mix until well combined. Add eggs and coconut extract and mix until well combined. Add flour mixture in 3 additions, alternating with the coconut milk. Pour batter into the prepared pan and bake for 40-45 minutes, or until an inserted toothpick comes out clean. Cool coconut bread in the pan for 10 minutes, then invert onto a cooling rack set over a baking sheet.

While the bread bakes, make the glaze. In a medium skillet over medium heat, add shredded coconut. Toast coconut, stirring occasionally, until lightly browned, about 5 minutes. Pour coconut onto a plate to cool and set aside. In a small bowl, combine powdered sugar, coconut milk and coconut extract. Whisk well until smooth and set aside.

While the bread is still warm, pour glaze over the baked bread on the cooling rack, with the baking sheet catching the drips. Sprinkle the toasted coconut on top.

Toasted Garlic Bread

Isn't it a tragedy when you are served a big, steaming plate of spaghetti and there is no garlic bread? No partner in crime when it comes to sopping up all the leftover marinara sauce. No crisp, buttery bread loaded with garlic goodness? Sad. Just sad.

Yields 8 servings

½ cup unsalted butter, softened
¼ cup freshly grated Parmesan cheese
5 garlic cloves, minced
1½ teaspoons dried Italian seasoning blend
½ teaspoon kosher salt
1 long French bread loaf, sliced in half lengthwise

Set broiler to low. In a small bowl, combine butter, Parmesan, garlic, Italian seasoning blend and salt. Mix until well combined. Spread butter mixture on the cut side of each half of the French bread. Set bread halves, cut side up, on a baking sheet. Put under the broiler and broil until butter is melted and bread is lightly toasted, about 5 minutes.

Transfer bread to a cutting board and slice bread into portions.

Pictured on Page 131.

Homemade Croutons

I have been known to have my sisters take the crouton oath. It goes as follows: "I (your name) hereby swear I will never buy croutons ever again because they are a waste of money and not that good. I will forever make my own." Take the oath and see why I consider homemade croutons such a critical issue. What's great about croutons is that you can use any bread. Whenever we have leftover french bread, dinner rolls or hamburger buns, I freeze them and use them as croutons later.

Yields 6 servings

3 tablespoons extra virgin olive oil
8 cups cubed bread, fresh or stale
½ teaspoon kosher salt
¼ teaspoon ground pepper

In a large skillet over medium heat, add olive oil. Once the oil is heated, add bread cubes, salt and pepper. Toss well. Cook bread cubes, stirring occasionally, until lightly browned, about 15-20 minutes. Pour onto a plate and allow croutons to cool. Serve in a salad or soup.

Desserts

Sheena's Chocolate-Dipped Peanut Butter Cookies 203

Ginger Softie Cookies 204

Double Chocolate Cookies 205

Pecan Shortbread Bars 206

Karla's Buttermilk Cake with Whipped Cream & Strawberries 208

Elma's Double Chocolate Cake 210

Chocolate-Swirl Pumpkin Gingerbread 213

Tricia's Carrot Cake with Cream Cheese Frosting 214

Blackberry Crumble 217

Pat's Chocolate Cinnamon Sheet Cake 218

Crumb-Top Apple Pie 221

PB&J Rice Crispy Treats 222

Pineapple Sorbet with Strawberry Coconut Sauce 225

Raspberry Ice Cream with Cracked Chocolate 226

Spiced-Pear Cheesecake 228

Brownies 231

Lemon Cupcakes with Cream Cheese Frosting 232

Vanilla Cupcakes with Chocolate Buttercream 234

Maple Ice Cream 235

Blueberry Oatmeal Bars 237

Chocolate Cream Pie 238

Orange Cream Cake 241

Sheena's Chocolate-Dipped Peanut Butter Cookies
Ginger Softie Cookies, pg. 204
Double Chocolate Cookies, pg. 205

Sheena's Chocolate-Dipped Peanut Butter Cookies

Recipe by Sheena Jibson

Sheena is the one we can thank for the gorgeous photos in this book. And these cookies are her speciality. She mostly makes them to take on camping trips with her family. These aren't your typical peanut butter cookies; they are soft and cake-like, thanks to a bit of sour cream in the batter.

Yields 2½ dozen cookies

2 cups all-purpose flour
1 teaspoon baking powder
1 teaspoon salt
¼ teaspoon baking soda
¼ cup unsalted butter, softened
1 cup creamy peanut butter

½ cup brown sugar
½ cup granulated sugar
2 eggs
3 tablespoons sour cream
2 teaspoons pure vanilla extract
6 ounces semisweet chocolate, chopped

Set oven to 350 degrees F.

In a medium bowl, combine flour, baking powder, salt and baking soda. Whisk to combine and set aside.

In a mixing bowl fitted with the paddle attachment, combine butter, peanut butter, brown sugar and sugar and mix on medium speed until the mixture is light and fluffy, about 2 minutes. Add eggs, sour cream and vanilla extract and mix well, scraping the sides of the mixer with a rubber spatula. Add flour mixture and stir until well combined, but be sure not to overmix.

Portion cookie dough into small, 2-inch balls. Set on a baking sheet, 1-inch apart. Bake for 13-15 minutes, until the cookies are set in the middle and the edges are lightly browned. Once out of the oven, gently press the tops of the cookies down and flatten. Let cool on the baking sheet for 5 minutes, then transfer to a cooling rack. Repeat with remaining cookie dough.

While the cookies cool, melt the semisweet chocolate. In a double boiler, add the chocolate. Melt, stirring occasionally and then remove pan from heat. Lay a long sheet of waxed paper on the counter. Dip each cookie, only covering half of the cookie. Set on the waxed paper and let sit until the chocolate is set.

Ginger Softie Cookies

Our church services started at 9:00 a.m. I was busy putting on a final coat of lipstick and getting my son's church shoes on. As I filled up the sippy cup to put in the diaper bag, I spied my husband out of the corner of my eye. Was he shoving cookies in his suit jacket pocket? Oh my gosh! He was! And then an hour later, as church services were in full swing, there sits my husband, sneaking bites of ginger softies. But I wasn't mad, I was jealous. These babies are incredibly soft and moist and packed full of spice and molasses.

Yields 2 dozen cookies

2¼ cup all-purpose flour
2 teaspoons ground ginger
1 teaspoon baking soda
¾ teaspoon ground cinnamon
½ teaspoon ground cloves
¼ teaspoon ground nutmeg
¼ teaspoon salt
¾ cup unsalted butter, softened
1 cup granulated sugar, plus more for rolling the cookies
1 egg
¼ cup molasses

Set oven to 350 degrees F.
In a medium bowl, combine flour, ginger, baking soda, cinnamon, cloves, nutmeg and salt. Whisk to combine and set aside.

In a mixing bowl fitted with the paddle attachment, combine butter and sugar and mix on medium speed until the mixture is light and fluffy, about 2 minutes. Add egg and molasses and mix well, scraping the sides of the mixer with a rubber spatula. Add flour mixture and mix until well combined, but being sure to not overmix.
Pour a small amount of sugar into a small bowl. Portion cookie dough into small, 2 inch balls and roll in the sugar, completely coating them. Set on a baking sheet, 1-inch apart. Bake for 8-10 minutes, until the cookies are set in the middle. Let cool on the baking sheet for 5 minutes, then transfer to a cooling rack.

Pictured on Page 202.

Double Chocolate Cookies

Her feet are swollen, her belly rotund, and my sister Haley is in her last trimester of her pregnancy. She sits at my kitchen table, with weary hips and back, and asks for some cookies. How can I say no?! These are the cookies she requests: dark chocolate batter and gooey white chocolate chips. I wish I could credit my cookies for the beauty of her new baby girl.

Yields 2½ dozen cookies

2 cups all-purpose flour
½ cup unsweetened cocoa powder
¾ teaspoon baking soda
¼ teaspoon salt
1 cup unsalted butter, softened
1½ cups granulated sugar
2 eggs
1 teaspoon pure vanilla extract
2 cups white chocolate chips

Set oven to 350 degrees F.

In a medium bowl, combine flour, cocoa, baking soda and salt. Whisk to combine and set aside.

In a mixing bowl fitted with the paddle attachment, combine butter and sugar and mix on medium speed until the mixture is light and fluffy, about 2 minutes. Add eggs and vanilla extract and mix well, scraping the sides of the mixer with a rubber spatula. Add flour mixture and stir until just mixed. With the mixer running, add chocolate chips. Continue mixing until flour and chocolate chips are well combined, but being sure not to overmix.

Portion cookie dough into small, 2 inch balls. Set on a baking sheet, 1 inch apart. Bake for 10-12 minutes, until the cookies are set in the middle. Let cool on the baking sheet for 5 minutes, then transfer to a cooling rack.

Pictured on Page 202.

Pecan Shortbread Bars

These buttery, nutty Pecan Shortbread Bars are my 4 year old's favorite. He is my only child that likes to help in the kitchen and with these cookies, his job is to press the dough into the pan. Sure, it isn't always even, but if he is helping me in the kitchen, it's keeping him from pestering his older brother and little sister. Poor middle child can't catch a break.

Yields 18 cookies

1 cup pecans
1½ cups all-purpose flour
⅔ cup granulated sugar
1 teaspoon salt
¾ cup cold butter, cut into small pieces

Set oven to 325 degrees F.

In a medium saucepan over medium heat, add pecans. Toast pecans until they are fragrant and lightly toasted, about 5 minutes. Pour pecans into the bowl of a food processor and let cool. Once cooled, process until pecans are finely ground. Add flour, sugar and salt and process to combine. Add butter and pulse until mixture resembles coarse crumbs. Press dough into a 9x13-inch baking pan. Bake shortbread for 25-30 minutes, or until shortbread is lightly browned on the edges. Cool completely. Cut shortbread cookies into 18 squares.

Karla's Buttermilk Cake with Whipped Cream & Strawberries

Recipe by Karla Munson

Karla is a dear friend and one that can bake anything. Everyone should have a Karla. Brioche to croissants to sourdough bread to cupcakes. And she was kind enough to share her recipe for this perfect cake. It is fluffy and sweet and loves strawberries. It's the birthday cake of choice for my husband. This cake is both light and moist. Light from the use of cake flour, and moist from the baked cake being soaked in a syrup of sugar and water.

Yields 8 servings

For the cake:
2 cups cake flour
1 teaspoon baking powder
1 teaspoon baking soda
¾ teaspoon salt
½ cup unsalted butter, softened
1 cup granulated sugar
2 eggs
1 teaspoon pure vanilla extract
1 cup buttermilk

For the syrup:
½ cup granulated sugar
½ cup water

For the whipped cream:
2 cups heavy cream
½ cup powdered sugar
Sliced strawberries, for garnish

Set oven to 350 degrees F.

For the cake, spray two 9-inch round cake pans with non-stick spray. Line the bottoms with a 9-inch round of parchment paper. Spray the paper and set aside.

In a medium bowl, combine flour, baking powder, baking soda and salt. Whisk to combine and set aside. In your mixing bowl fitted with the paddle attachment, combine butter and sugar and beat at medium speed until light and fluffy. Add eggs, one at a time, mixing well after each addition. Stir in vanilla extract. Add the flour mixture in three additions, alternating with the buttermilk. Mix until well combined. Pour batter into the prepared pans and smooth the top. Bake for about 25-30 minutes, or until an inserted toothpick comes out clean.

While the cake bakes, make the syrup. In a small saucepan over medium high heat, combine ½ cup sugar and water. Simmer until sugar is dissolved and mixture is clear, making a simple syrup. Set saucepan aside and allow to cool.

Once the cakes are baked, cool in the pans on a cooling rack for 20 minutes. With the cake still in the pan, poke holes all over the top with a toothpick. Slowly and evenly pour the simple syrup over the top of the cakes. Let cakes sit until all the syrup gets soaked in and the cakes are completely cooled.

While the cakes cool, make the whipped cream. In a mixing bowl fitted with the paddle attachment, pour in heavy cream. Beat on medium speed until cream is frothy. Add in powdered sugar and continue to beat until cream is thickened and holds a stiff peak. Set one of the layers on a cake plate. Spread a small amount of whipped cream on top. Add second layer on top and spread on the remaining whipped cream. Top with sliced strawberries. Keep refrigerated until serving.

Elma's Double Chocolate Cake

Recipe by Elma Hall

I am a sucker for a family recipe. Recipes that make it to every family gathering. Recipes that are handed down through the years, and if they are handwritten, even better. This is one such recipe. It belongs to my sister's grandma in-law. While I know it as Elma's, she would claim it as her sister, Shar's. Either way, it is the only chocolate cake that goes in my oven and comes out perfect each time. It's chocolatey, but not too rich. It tastes delicious with any frosting you can imagine. Here I have it with chocolate frosting, because that is my favorite way. But, regardless of the frosting flavor you choose, this is truly the perfect chocolate cake.

Yields 8 servings

For the cake:
2¼ cups all-purpose flour
½ cup unsweetened cocoa powder
1½ teaspoons baking soda
¾ teaspoon salt
1½ cups granulated sugar
¾ cup vegetable oil
2 eggs
1½ cups boiling water
1½ teaspoons pure vanilla extract

For the frosting:
½ cup unsalted butter, softened
1 cup unsweetened cocoa powder, sifted
5 cups powdered sugar
Pinch of salt
⅔ cup milk
2 teaspoons pure vanilla extract

Set oven to 350 degrees F.

Spray two 9-inch round pans with non-stick spray and set aside.

In a medium bowl, combine flour, cocoa powder, baking soda and salt. Whisk to combine and set aside. In a mixing bowl fitted with the paddle attachment, combine sugar, oil and eggs and mix at medium speed until combined. Add the flour mixture in three additions, alternating with the boiling water. Mix until well combined. Stir in 1½ teaspoons vanilla extract. Pour batter into prepared pans. Bake for 20-25 minutes, or until an inserted toothpick comes out clean. Allow cakes to cool for 20 minutes and then invert onto a cooling rack. Set aside to cool completely.

While the cakes cool, make the frosting. In a mixing bowl, combine butter, cocoa powder and powdered sugar and mix until butter is smooth. Add milk and vanilla extract. Adjust with more milk or powdered sugar if needed.

Line a cake plate with strips of waxed paper or parchment paper. Set one cake on top, being sure all plate surfaces are covered by paper. Spoon 1/4 of the frosting onto the cake and spread evenly with an off-set spatula or a butter knife. Top with the other cake. Spoon remaining frosting on top and spread, carefully spreading down and around the sides of the cakes. Gently remove paper from around the bottom of the cake.

Chocolate-Swirl Pumpkin Gingerbread

Gingerbread is great, sure. But what about gingerbread brought together with trusty chocolate and reliable pumpkin? Reliable pumpkin? Absolutely. Pumpkin will always put you in an autumn mood. Even if you live in a summer climate year round, have something pumpkin in the fall and you will undoubtedly feel like you are in New England crunching leaves under your boots and wearing a scarf. This cake will do that very thing.

Yields 8 servings

4 ounces semisweet chocolate, roughly chopped
2 cups all purpose flour
2 teaspoons baking powder
2 teaspoons baking soda
1½ teaspoons ground cinnamon
¾ teaspoon ground ginger
½ teaspoon salt

½ cup butter, softened
1 cup granulated sugar
2 eggs
½ cup molasses
½ cup pumpkin puree
½ cup boiling water

Set oven to 350 degrees F.

Spray a 9x13-inch pan with non-stick spray and set aside. In a double boiler, add the chocolate. Melt, stirring occasionally and then remove pan from heat, leaving the bowl on the double boiler to keep the chocolate melted.

In a medium bowl, combine flour, baking powder, baking soda, cinnamon, ginger and salt. Whisk to combine and set aside. In a mixing bowl fitted with a paddle attachment, combine sugar and butter and beat on medium speed until light and fluffy, about 2 minutes. Add eggs, one at a time, mixing well after each addition. Stir in molasses and pumpkin. Stir in the boiling water. With a rubber scraper, fold in flour mixture.

Pour half the batter into the prepared pan. Pour in half the melted chocolate in an "S" pattern. Pour on the remaining batter, then top with the remaining chocolate. Run a butter knife through the batter to better swirl the chocolate, but do not fully incorporate.

Bake for 35-40 minutes or until an inserted toothpick comes out clean.

Tricia's Carrot Cake with Cream Cheese Frosting

Recipe by Tricia Swift-Buggle

This cake was a cake of legend in my church group in Southern California. My friend, Tricia, would bring it to gatherings and it would disappear as quickly as it came in the door. It holds a special memory for me because it was brought to my baby shower for my second baby. I remember being around 8 months pregnant, feet up, and eating a huge slice of this. Happiest memory a pregnant woman can have. Moist-as-can-be cake covered in sweet, creamy frosting. It's one of those cakes that tastes better as the days go by, if it ever makes it that long.

Yields 8 servings

For the cake:

2¼ cups all-purpose flour

1 teaspoon baking soda

1 teaspoon salt

1 teaspoon ground cinnamon

1¾ cups granulated sugar

1¼ cups vegetable oil

4 eggs

½ teaspoon pure vanilla extract

1 8 ounce can crushed pineapple, drained

3 cups grated carrots

1 cup raisins

1 cup chopped walnuts,
plus additional for garnish

For the frosting:

12 ounces cream cheese, softened

¾ cup unsalted butter, softened

1½ teaspoons pure vanilla extract

5 cups powdered sugar

Set oven to 375 degrees F.

Spray two 9-inch round cake pans with non-stick spray and set aside.

In a medium bowl, combine flour, baking soda, salt and cinnamon. Whisk to combine and set aside. In a mixing bowl fitted with the paddle attachment, combine sugar and oil and mix at medium speed until combined. Add eggs, one at a time, mixing well after each addition.

Stir in vanilla. Add the flour mixture and mix until just combined. Stir in pineapple, carrots, raisins and walnuts.

Pour batter into prepared pans and smooth the top. Bake for 35-40 minutes, or until an inserted toothpick comes out clean. Allow cakes to cool for 20 minutes and then invert onto a cooling rack. Once cooled, refrigerate for 2 hours before spreading on frosting.

Once the cakes have been refrigerated, make the frosting. In a mixing bowl, combine cream cheese, butter and vanilla extract and mix until well combined. Add powdered sugar and mix until smooth.

Line a cake plate with strips of waxed or parchment paper. Set one cake on top, being sure all plate surfaces are covered by paper. Spoon ¼ of the frosting onto the cake and spread evenly with an off-set spatula or a butter knife. Top with other cake. Spoon remaining frosting on top and spread, carefully spreading down and around the sides of the cakes. Gently remove paper from around the cake. Garnish cake with walnuts. Refrigerate until serving.

Blackberry Crumble

Have you ever been blackberry picking? It is easily one of the most delicious things you can do. No blackberry can ever taste as good as one fresh off the bush, warmed by the sun. More end up in my mouth than in my bucket. For the ones that have the great fortune of making it home, this is what I do with them. Blackberries topped with a nutty crumble and baked until the berries burst. And can you guess who likes blackberry crumble almost as much as I do? Vanilla ice cream.

Yields 8 servings

¾ cup all-purpose flour
¾ cup quick-cooking or old-fashioned oats
½ cup chopped pecans
¼ cup brown sugar
¾ teaspoon ground cinnamon
½ teaspoon salt
¼ cup unsalted butter, melted
6 cups fresh blackberries
1 tablespoon cornstarch
1 tablespoon granulated sugar
Vanilla ice cream, for serving

Set the oven to 375 degrees F.

In a medium bowl, combine the flour, oats, pecans, brown sugar, cinnamon and salt. Add the butter and mix well until combined. Set aside.

In an 8x8-inch pan, combine blackberries, cornstarch and sugar. Gently toss to combine. Spread evenly. Sprinkle the flour mixture on top and gently press it down, being sure to go all the way to the edges.

Set pan on a baking sheet and bake for 50 minutes. Allow to cool for 10 minutes before serving. Serve with a scoop of vanilla ice cream.

Pat's Chocolate Cinnamon Sheet Cake
Recipe by Pat Segal

You all wish you had your very own Pat. She is a wealth of knowledge, having graduated from Le Cordon Bleu in Pasadena, specializing in pastry. She is so generous with her delicious talents. She was the one that helped me win the church chili competition and she also sat at my house for hours and hours as we made a real Christmas gingerbread house. Pat is about as wonderful as they come. Here is one of her kids' favorites. Incredibly moist chocolate cake with a hint of cinnamon, and covered in rich, smooth chocolate icing. She says that when she goes to Louisiana to visit her son, he requests she makes two of these before she leaves.

Yields 8 servings

For the cake:
2 cups all-purpose flour
2 cups granulated sugar
1½ teaspoons ground cinnamon
1 teaspoon baking soda
½ teaspoon salt
2 eggs
½ cup buttermilk
1 teaspoon pure vanilla extract
1 cup water
½ cup unsalted butter
¼ cup vegetable shortening
¼ cup unsweetened cocoa powder

For the icing:
3½ cups powdered sugar
½ cup unsalted butter
½ cup buttermilk
¼ cup unsweetened cocoa powder
1 teaspoon ground cinnamon

Set oven to 350 degrees F.

Spray a 13x18-inch baking sheet with non-stick spray and set aside.

In a mixing bowl fitted with the paddle attachment, add flour, sugar, cinnamon, baking soda and salt. Mix until well combined and set aside. In a small bowl, combine the eggs, buttermilk and vanilla. Whisk and set aside.

In a medium saucepan over medium high heat, combine the water, butter, shortening and cocoa powder. Stir occasionally, until the butter and shortening are melted. Remove from heat and pour the chocolate mixture into the flour mixture. Add the eggs and buttermilk mixture and mix at medium speed until combined. Pour into the prepared sheet pan. Bake for 15-20 minutes, or until an inserted toothpick comes out clean.

While the cake bakes, make the icing. In the mixing bowl, add powdered sugar and set aside. In the medium saucepan over medium high heat, combine cocoa powder, butter, buttermilk and cinnamon. Stir occasionally, until the butter is melted. Remove from heat and pour chocolate mixture into the powdered sugar and mix on medium speed until combined. Spread over warm cake. Cool completely before serving.

Crumb-Top Apple Pie
Maple Ice Cream, pg. 235

Crumb-Top Apple Pie

Apple pie is always my Thanksgiving offering. This pie is much less daunting than an apple pie with a pastry top crust. I always seem to screw up the top crust. I get nervous and my hands get all hot and clammy, which is enemy number one of a good pie crust. This pie is perfect for me. A topping full of cinnamon and butter that sits atop tart apples. Simple and, well, easy as pie.

Yields 8 servings

For the filling:

1 recipe for a pie crust for a 9-inch pie pan, store-bought or homemade

6 Granny Smith apples, peeled, cored and thinly sliced

1 tablespoon fresh lemon juice
½ cup brown sugar
2 tablespoons all-purpose flour
1 teaspoon ground cinnamon
½ teaspoon ground nutmeg
¼ teaspoon salt

For the crumb topping:

1 cup all-purpose flour
½ cup granulated sugar
2 tablespoons brown sugar
½ teaspoon ground cinnamon
½ cup unsalted butter, cut into cubes
½ cup chopped pecans

Set oven to 400 degrees F.

Roll out pie crust and place in a 9-inch pie plate. Crimp edges and set pie crust in refrigerator.

In a large bowl, combine apples, lemon juice, brown sugar, flour, cinnamon, nutmeg and salt. Toss well, being sure all apples are coated with brown sugar. Set aside and allow the apples to macerate.

While the apples macerate, make the crumb topping. In the bowl of a food processor, combine flour, sugar, brown sugar and cinnamon. Pulse until combined. Add butter and pulse until mixture resembles sand, about 20 pulses. Pour crumb topping into a medium bowl and stir in pecans.

Remove pie crust from the refrigerator. Pour apples into the pie crust and carefully pour crumb topping on top, pressed down to pack it on top of the apples. Set pie pan on a baking sheet and bake for 40 minutes, until crust is golden. Remove pie from the oven and carefully wrap foil around the crust to protect it from further browning. Set pie back in the oven, reduce heat to 350 degrees F and bake pie for an additional 40 minutes.

Cool pie completely or serve warm.

PB&J Rice Crispy Treats

Here is a double throwback to childhood. Both rice crispy treats and peanut butter and jelly come together to produce a sticky, sweet treat sure to remind you of the foods of your youth. What would these treats be good for? Well, lunch while on a hike, an offering at the office potluck, dessert for the neighborhood barbecue, a package sent to a college student, refreshment for a slumber party or even a soccer team reward ... to name a few. Anywhere you take these, everyone will get a healthy dose of childhood memory.

Yields 12 servings

8 cups crispy rice cereal
6 tablespoons unsalted butter
½ teaspoon salt
6 cups mini marshmallows
¾ cup smooth peanut butter
⅓ cup fruit jam

Pour crispy rice cereal into a large bowl and set aside.

In a large saucepan over medium high heat, add butter and salt. Once butter is melted, stir in marshmallows and stir constantly until marshmallows are melted and the mixture is smooth. Remove pan from heat and stir in peanut butter until smooth.

Pour mixture over crispy rice cereal and mix well, until all cereal is coated. Spray your hands with non-stick spray and press half of the crispy rice treats into the bottom of a 9x13-inch pan. Spread jam evenly on top and then top the jam layer with the other half of the crispy rice treats. Let crispy rice treats set for 30 minutes. Cut into squares and serve.

Pineapple Sorbet with Strawberry Coconut Sauce

Dole Whip. That creamy, dreamy, frozen heaven-in-a-cup sold by the Tiki Room in Disneyland. It's tart but sweet and the most perfect remedy for a steaming hot summer day at the Happiest Place on Earth or as I call it, "The Happiest Place on Earth For World-Class People Watching."

This sorbet is as luscious as Dole Whip. But to make it better, drizzle it with some strawberry coconut sauce. It's quite reminiscent of a lava flow and quite delicious. P.S. Look for cream of coconut by the drink mixers in the grocery store.

Yields 6 servings

4 cups chopped pineapple
1 cup granulated sugar
1 cup water
1 pound strawberries, hulled
½ cup cream of coconut

In a blender, combine pineapple, sugar and water. Blend until smooth. Pour mixture into a bowl, tightly cover with plastic and set in fridge for at least 6 hours or overnight.

In the blender, combine strawberries and cream of coconut. Blend until smooth. Pour into a small bowl and set in the fridge.

Once the pineapple mixture is thoroughly chilled, churn in an ice cream maker according to manufacturer's instructions. Serve immediately or transfer sorbet to an airtight container and freeze until solid.

Serve sorbet with strawberry coconut sauce drizzled over the top.

Raspberry Ice Cream with Cracked Chocolate

I still remember the day my ice cream maker came in the mail. As I pulled my car into my garage, I saw it sitting on my front porch. I quickly brought it inside and cut the tape on the box. As I pulled the shiny silver ice cream maker out of its box, I could swear I heard it whisper, "You and I are going to make magic together." And make magic we did. How I lived so long without the glory of homemade ice cream, I do not know. A small amount of effort yields a tasty treat that stays good in the freezer for weeks, if it even lasts that long. This ice cream isn't going to last long, I can tell you that right now. Plenty of raspberries mixed in a thick custard and dotted with chocolate are sure to disappear quickly.

===========

Yields 6 servings

2 cups heavy cream
½ teaspoon pure vanilla extract
4 cups fresh or frozen raspberries, thawed
5 egg yolks

1½ cups half and half
1 cup granulated sugar
8 ounces semisweet chocolate, finely chopped

===========

In a large bowl, add heavy cream and set a fine wire mesh strainer over the top and set aside. In a food processor or blender, add raspberries and process until smooth. Pour raspberry puree into the wire mesh strainer and press puree through the strainer into the heavy cream. Discard seeds, rinse out the strainer and set it back on the bowl. Set raspberry mixture aside. In a large bowl, add egg yolks and whisk until smooth. Set aside.

In a large saucepan over medium heat, add half and half and sugar. Stir often, until steam rises from the mixture and is hot to the touch. Remove pan from heat and slowly pour half-and-half mixture into the egg yolks, whisking constantly. Pour egg yolk and half-and-half mixture back into the saucepan and return to the heat. Stir mixture constantly with a wooden spoon, until thickened and it coats the back of the spoon well. Remove pan from heat and pour into the raspberry mixture through wire-mesh strainer. Set bowl into an ice water bath. Stir mixture occasionally, until cooled. Cover tightly with plastic wrap and set in the fridge overnight.

While ice cream base chills in the fridge, melt chocolate in a double boiler, stirring occasionally. Line a baking sheet with waxed paper. Once all chocolate is melted, pour chocolate onto the waxed paper and spread into a thin layer. Set baking sheet in the freezer and freeze until chocolate is firm, about 15 minutes. Remove chocolate from freezer and fold the waxed paper in half to break the chocolate. With a skillet or a mallet, break the chocolate into bite-sized shards. Transfer cracked chocolate into a small bowl and set chocolate back in the freezer.

Once thoroughly chilled, churn ice cream base in an ice cream maker according to manufacturer's instructions. Transfer ice cream to an airtight container, stir in cracked chocolate and freeze until solid.

Spiced-Pear Cheesecake

Here is what you are bringing for your Thanksgiving offering. A fall dessert worthy of sharing a table with a turkey. All the flavors of fall are right in this cheesecake. Cinnamon, ginger, nutmeg and juicy pears. It will be a nice change to the usual pumpkin pie. Not that I am speaking from experience, but a slice of this makes a great breakfast.

Yields 8 servings

For the crust:
2 cups graham cracker crumbs
½ cup unsalted butter, melted

For the cheesecake:
4 cups peeled and diced pears
½ cup granulated sugar
1 cup water
4 8 ounce packages cream cheese, softened

1 cup granulated sugar
2 eggs
4 egg yolks
1½ teaspoons pure vanilla extract
1 teaspoon ground cinnamon
½ teaspoon ground nutmeg
½ teaspoon ground ginger
¼ teaspoon ground cloves
Boiling water, for water bath

Set oven to 350 degrees F.

In a medium bowl, combine graham cracker crumbs and butter. Mix until well combined. Press into the bottom and 1 inch up the sides of a 9-inch springform pan. Bake for 10 minutes until lightly browned. Set aside to cool. Once cooled, rip off two large pieces of aluminum foil and set on the counter in an X shape. Set the springform pan in the middle. Bring foil up around the sides of the pan, being sure to cover the bottom well to prevent water from the water bath leaking in.

In a medium saucepan over medium high heat, add pears, sugar and water. Simmer, while mashing with a potato masher occasionally, until liquid is reduced and pears are the consistency of applesauce, about 20 minutes. Remove pan from heat and pour into a medium bowl and refrigerate until completely cooled.

In a mixing bowl fitted with the whisk attachment, add cream cheese and whisk on medium until smooth. Add sugar, eggs, egg yolks, vanilla extract, cinnamon, nutmeg, ginger and cloves and whisk on medium high speed until mixture is completely smooth and no lumps remain, about 5 minutes. Fold in cooled pear mixture. Pour over cooled graham cracker crust. Set cheesecake inside a large pan big enough for a water bath, like a roasting pan and add boiling water until it reaches halfway up the springform pan.

With the oven still at 350 degrees F, bake for 1 hour and 15 minutes, until center is firm, but still jiggles slightly. Turn off heat and wedge open the oven door with a wooden spoon and let cheesecake cool completely in the oven, about 3 hours. Refrigerate overnight. Serve chilled.

Brownies

I used to have a saying: "I can make a cake better than a cake mix, but I can't make a brownie better than a brownie mix." But being the kind of gal I am, I couldn't leave well enough alone and I embarked on the voyage of making the from-scratch brownie of my dreams. These ladies are chocolatey and rich, but not overly gooey or sweet. My secret? Just a bit of cake flour.

Yields 9 brownies

¾ cup all-purpose flour
½ cup cake flour
½ cup unsweetened cocoa powder
¾ teaspoon baking powder
½ teaspoon salt
¾ cup unsalted butter, chopped
6 ounces semi-sweet chocolate, chopped
1½ cups granulated sugar
3 eggs
1½ teaspoons pure vanilla extract

Set oven to 325 degrees F.

Spray an 8x8-inch pan with non-stick spray. Line the pan with a strip of parchment paper, allowing for a 2-inch overhang on each side. Spray the parchment and set aside. In a medium bowl, combine all-purpose flour, cake flour, cocoa powder, baking powder and salt. Whisk to combine and set aside.

In a double boiler over simmering water, add butter and chocolate. Melt over medium heat, stirring occasionally, until smooth. Remove bowl from over the water and stir sugar into chocolate mixture. Mix well until combined. Stir in eggs, one at a time, until well combined. Stir in vanilla extract. Stir in half of the flour mixture until well combined and then stir in the other half.

Pour brownie batter into the prepared pan. Bake for 45-50 minutes, or until an inserted toothpick comes out with a few moist crumbs attached. Allow to cool for 1 hour. Remove brownies from the pan using the parchment overhang. Slice into nine squares.

Lemon Cupcakes with Cream Cheese Frosting

It's time for a super moist, sweet and tart cupcake with cream cheese frosting smeared on top. These cupcakes and their lightness are perfect for a summer cookout or maybe after Easter dinner. Something about lemon reminds me of summer. Maybe it's the lemonade that makes me think that. Or maybe I am reminded of my in-law's lemon tree. Either way, these cupcakes would turn any spring or summer event into a really sweet one.

Yields 12 cupcakes

For the cupcakes:

1½ cups all-purpose flour
1½ teaspoons baking powder
½ teaspoon baking soda
½ teaspoon salt
½ cup unsalted butter, softened
¾ cup granulated sugar
2 eggs
¼ cup sour cream
1 teaspoon pure vanilla extract
¼ cup milk
2 lemons, zested and juiced

For the frosting:

⅓ cup unsalted butter, softened
6 ounces cream cheese, softened
1 teaspoon pure vanilla extract
3¾ cups powdered sugar
2 teaspoons milk

Set oven to 350 degrees F.

Line a 12-cup muffin pan with liners and set aside.

In a medium bowl, combine flour, baking powder, baking soda and salt. Whisk to combine and set aside. In a mixing bowl fitted with the paddle attachment, combine butter and sugar and beat until light and fluffy. Add eggs, one at a time, mixing well after each addition. Stir in sour cream and vanilla extract. Add the flour mixture in three additions, alternating with the milk. Stir in ¼ cup of the fresh lemon juice and all the zest. Mix until well combined.

Divide batter between cupcake liners. Bake for 18-20 minutes, or until an inserted toothpick comes out clean. Cool completely.

While the cupcakes cool, make the frosting. In a mixing bowl fitted with the whisk attachment, combine butter, cream cheese and vanilla extract and mix until combined. Add powdered sugar and milk and mix on medium speed until smooth. Spread cheese frosting on top of each cupcake.

Lemon Cupcakes with Cream Cheese Frosting
Vanilla Cupcakes with Chocolate Buttercream, Pg. 234

Vanilla Cupcakes with Chocolate Buttercream

Cupcakes and I, we need to keep our distance from each other. It's not Cupcake's fault, it's all mine. I abuse our relationship. I take Cupcake for granted, especially if Chocolate is involved. It's just not a healthy relationship. The honest truth is that I can eat the whole dozen, even if I don't put my mind to it. I just do it. These babies are maybe my worst offense. Moist, vanilla-flavored cupcakes topped with rich, smooth chocolate buttercream. Someone come intervene!

Yields 12 cupcakes

For the cupcakes:

1½ cups all-purpose flour
1½ teaspoons baking powder
½ teaspoon baking soda
½ teaspoon salt
½ cup unsalted butter, softened
¾ cup granulated sugar
2 eggs
¼ cup sour cream
1½ teaspoons pure vanilla extract
¼ cup milk

For the buttercream:

6 tablespoons unsalted butter, softened
¾ cup unsweetened cocoa powder, sifted
4¼ cups powdered sugar
1½ teaspoons pure vanilla extract
½ cup milk

Set oven to 350 degrees F.

Line a 12-cup muffin pan with liners and set aside.

In a medium bowl, combine flour, baking powder, baking soda and salt. Whisk to combine and set aside. In a mixing bowl fitted with the paddle attachment, combine butter and sugar and beat until light and fluffy. Add eggs, one at a time, mixing well after each addition. Stir in sour cream and vanilla extract. Add the flour mixture in three additions, alternating with the milk. Mix until well combined.

Divide batter between cupcake liners. Bake for 18-20 minutes, or until an inserted toothpick comes out clean. Cool completely.

While the cupcakes cool, make the buttercream. In a mixing bowl fitted with the whisk attachment, combine butter, cocoa powder, powdered sugar and vanilla extract and mix until combined. Add milk and mix on medium speed until smooth. Adjust with more milk or powdered sugar if needed. Spread or pipe chocolate buttercream on top of each cupcake.

Pictured on Page 233.

Maple Ice Cream

Creamy, thick and perfectly sweetened with only maple syrup. And let's be clear, I am talking about pure maple syrup. The good stuff that is tapped from a tree. Pure maple syrup can get a little pricey, but Amazon.com has great prices on the stuff. A quick tip on making ice cream: use your kitchen sink to be your ice water bath. Fill up the sink with cold water and a bunch of ice. Do that and then you aren't using yet another bowl.

Yields 6 servings

2 cups heavy cream
¼ teaspoon pure vanilla extract
5 egg yolks
1 cup pure maple syrup
1½ cups half and half

In a large bowl, pour in heavy cream and vanilla extract and set a wire mesh strainer over the top. Set aside. In a large bowl add egg yolks and whisk well. Set aside.

In a large saucepan over medium heat, add maple syrup. Simmer, stirring occasionally, for 5 minutes, until syrup is reduced by half. Remove pan from heat and let cool for a few minutes. Return pan to heat and stir in half and half. Stir often, until steam rises from the mixture and it is hot to the touch. Remove pan from heat and very slowly pour half-and-half mixture into the egg yolks, whisking constantly. Pour egg yolk and half-and-half mixture back into the saucepan and return to the heat. Stir mixture constantly with a wooden spoon, until thickened and it coats the back of the spoon well. Remove pan from heat and pour into heavy cream through wire-mesh strainer. Remove strainer and set bowl into an ice water bath. Stir mixture occasionally, until cooled. Cover tightly with plastic wrap and set in the fridge overnight.

Once thoroughly chilled, churn ice cream base in an ice cream maker according to manufacturer's instructions. Transfer ice cream to an airtight container and freeze until solid.

Pictured on Page 220.

Blueberry Oatmeal Bars

Like most people, blueberries always remind me of "Willy Wonka and the Chocolate Factory." You know, when Violet Beauregarde eats the gum and starts to blow up and become a giant blueberry. "Violet! You're turning violet, Violet!" A bonus for me though, is that my daughter is named Violet. As you can imagine, we say that to her all the time. These treats are a perfect way to employ blueberries. Crisp crust, bright violet filling and just the right amount of sweetness. They hold up especially well in lunchboxes.

Yields 9 servings

For the filling:

2 cups fresh or thawed frozen blueberries
⅓ cup granulated sugar
2 teaspoons fresh lemon juice
1 tablespoon cornstarch
1 tablespoon water
½ teaspoon pure vanilla extract

For the crust and topping:

1¼ cup all-purpose flour
¾ cup quick-cooking or old-fashioned oats
½ cup brown sugar
¼ teaspoon baking soda
¼ teaspoon salt
½ cup unsalted butter, melted

Set oven to 350 degrees F.

In a medium saucepan over medium high heat, add blueberries, sugar and lemon juice. Mix well to combine. Simmer for 5 minutes, or until most of the blueberries have popped and released their juices. In a small bowl, combine cornstarch and water and stir well to combine. Remove pan from the heat and stir in the cornstarch mixture and vanilla extract. Stir well to combine and set aside.

In a mixing bowl fitted with a paddle attachment, add flour, oats, brown sugar, baking soda, salt and butter. Mix on medium speed until well combined. Press ¾ of the mixture into the bottom of an 8x8-inch pan. Pour the blueberry filling on top and then sprinkle the remaining oat mixture on top of that. Bake for 30-35 minutes, or until the top is golden brown. Cool completely and cut into squares.

Chocolate Cream Pie

My father in-law is a pie lover. It's pie that holds his birthday candles, not cake. When I see a Marie Callender's box, I always think of him and family dinners, picnics or campouts. I have spent many evenings sitting around my in-laws' kitchen table, laughing and chatting, everyone with forks and all of us digging out bites straight from the pie plate. Chocolate cream happens to be his favorite. That cold, smooth chocolate filling and fresh whipped cream--it's pie heaven for my good ol' dad in-law.

Yields 6 servings

For the pie:

⅓ cup granulated sugar
2 tablespoons cornstarch
2 tablespoons unsweetened cocoa powder
⅛ teaspoon salt
1 cup milk
1 cup heavy cream
4 ounces semi-sweet chocolate, chopped
1 teaspoon pure vanilla extract
1 prepared 9-inch graham cracker pie crust,
store-bought or homemade, cooled completely

For the whipped cream:

1 cup heavy cream
¼ cup powdered sugar

In a large saucepan, combine sugar, cornstarch, cocoa powder and salt. Whisk to combine and set heat to medium. Whisk in milk and heavy cream and bring to a boil, stirring occasionally. Once boiling, whisk constantly for 30 seconds. Add chocolate and boil for 2 more minutes, whisking constantly. Remove pan from heat and whisk in vanilla extract. Set aside to cool for 5 minutes, whisking occasionally. Pour chocolate filling into the pie shell and smooth the top. Set a sheet of plastic wrap directly on top of the chocolate filling, gently pressing down and being sure all surfaces are covered with plastic. Refrigerate until chocolate filling is set, about 6 hours.

Once the pie is set, make the whipped cream. In a mixing bowl fitted with the paddle attachment, pour in heavy cream. Beat on medium speed until cream is frothy. Add in powdered sugar and continue to beat until cream is thickened and holds a stiff peak. Remove the plastic wrap from the pie and spread whipped cream over the top of the chocolate cream pie. Serve chilled.

Orange Cream Cake

Let's, for just a second, talk about my inability to properly grease and flour a bundt pan. How many times have my bundt cakes cemented themselves into the pan, unwilling to slide out because I was too lazy to prepare the pan correctly? So many times! What ends up happening is that they eventually yield to my angry cursing and they fall out of the pan in pieces. And then I end up puzzling everything back together, trying to hide my mistakes. Learn from me! Grease that bundt pan and flour it! Take the time to do it right so you can avoid swearing at an innocent cake!

Yields 8 servings

For the cake:

3 cups all-purpose flour
2 teaspoons baking powder
1 teaspoon salt
½ teaspoon baking soda
1 cup unsalted butter, softened
2 cups granulated sugar
4 eggs

1 teaspoon pure vanilla extract
2 navel oranges, zested and juiced
1¼ cups heavy cream

For the orange syrup:

½ cup granulated sugar
½ cup orange juice

Set oven to 350 degrees F.

Spray a bundt pan with non-stick spray, dust with flour and set aside.

In a medium bowl, combine flour, baking powder, salt and baking soda. Whisk to combine and set aside. In a mixing bowl fit with the paddle attachment, combine butter and sugar and mix at medium speed until light and fluffy, about 2 minutes. Add eggs, one at a time, mixing well after each addition. Stir in vanilla extract and orange zest. Add the flour mixture in three additions, alternating with the heavy cream. Spoon batter into the prepared pan and smooth the top. Bake for 50-55 minutes, or until an inserted toothpick comes out clean.

While the cake bakes, make the orange syrup. In a small bowl, combine sugar and orange juice. Mix well. Once the cake is baked, poke holes all over the top with a toothpick. Slowly pour the syrup over the top. Once the syrup is absorbed, turn the cake out onto a cooling rack and allow to cool completely. Serve with fresh whipped cream.

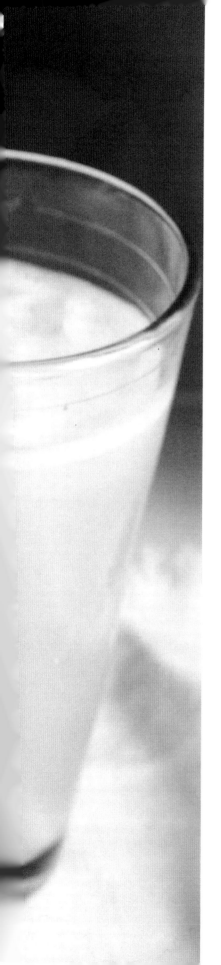

Drinks

Slow-Cooker Spiced Cider 244

Cantaloupe Agua Fresca 245

Dark Hot Chocolate & Ice Cream 246

Frozen Lemonade 247

Slow-Cooker Spiced Cider

This apple cider always reminds me of my sister in-law, Jacque. Although she lives in sunny Southern California, she embraces all things Fall with complete dedication. Her Fall decor rivals the most fancy Christmas decor you have ever seen. Pumpkin all of a sudden becomes a daily staple. And she hosts her annual Witch's Brew Party. I suppose it would be appropriate to dedicate this recipe to her. So I shall. Jacque, this one's for you!

Yields 8 servings

1 gallon apple cider
1 navel orange, halved
1 teaspoon ground cinnamon
¼ teaspoon ground nutmeg
5 whole cloves

Pour apple cider into the slow cooker. Add orange, cinnamon, nutmeg and cloves. Stir well. Cook on high for 4 hours. Before serving, remove orange and cloves with a slotted spoon.

Cantaloupe Agua Fresca

I like to think of this as grownup Kool-Aid. A pretty orange color, not too sweet and made with real fruit. I can imagine that this would taste especially delicious in the afternoon while my two littles take naps. Maybe with a great book and a brownie? And someone giving me a pedicure? And possibly a scalp massage? Oh boy, I have gotten off track.

Yields 6 servings
6 cups chopped cantaloupe melon
½ cup granulated sugar
2 tablespoons fresh lemon juice
4 cups water

Set a fine wire mesh strainer over a large bowl and set aside.

In the bowl of a food processor, add half of the cantaloupe, ¼ cup sugar and 1 tablespoon lemon juice. Process until smooth. Pour cantaloupe mixture into the strainer. Let mixture drain. Pour liquid into a pitcher and discard the pulp. Repeat process with the other half of cantaloupe chunks. Add the water to the cantaloupe mixture and stir well. Refrigerate and serve cold over ice.

Pictured on Page 109.

Dark Hot Chocolate & Ice Cream

A few years ago, my hot chocolate life was changed. My cousin's wife, Janeen, told me of this legend. A legend of people putting a scoop of vanilla ice cream in their hot chocolate. I was astonished. I could imagine the joy of lava-hot hot chocolate melting frozen vanilla ice cream, adding its creamy sweetness and making what once was a drink, a dessert. She then said this is what she gives her children after a day in the snow! It wasn't legend! It was true! You must try this. It's a heavenly winter dessert.

Yields 6 servings

1 cup half and half
3½ cups milk
½ cup granulated sugar
6 ounces bittersweet chocolate, finely chopped
Vanilla ice cream, for serving

In a medium saucepan over medium heat, add half and half, milk and sugar. Bring to a gentle simmer, stirring occasionally. Once simmering, whisk in chocolate. Whisk until chocolate is melted.

Set out six mugs. Add a scoop of vanilla ice cream to each one. Fill each mug with hot chocolate and serve.

Frozen Lemonade

My in-laws have a lemon tree in their backyard. When we go down to California to visit, I always bring home a box of lemons. Our car is already crammed full, but somehow I am always able to "Tetris" in a box of lemons. I bring the lemons home and treat my family to a few solid days of lemony delights, both savory and sweet. Lemon bars, lemon chicken and rice, lemon blueberry muffins and this: frozen lemonade. It's like a lemonade Slurpee. A bit of Southern California sun in a glass.

Yields 6 servings

1 cup freshly squeezed lemon juice
1 cup granulated sugar
3 cups water
12 ice cubes

In a blender, combine lemon juice, sugar and water. Blend until sugar is dissolved. Pour lemon mixture into a pitcher. Add ice into the blender and blend until ice is crushed and like snow. Divide ice between six glasses. Pour lemonade over the top. Serve immediately with a straw.

Pictured on Page 132.

ABOUT THE AUTHOR:

Whitney Ingram

Besides spending way too much time in the kitchen, Whitney enjoys a good run, a good book and a big plate of good Mexican food. Whitney lives in Utah with her husband and three small children and they own Rockwell Catering and Events. "The Family Flavor" is her first book. For questions about this cookbook, please contact Whitney at thefamilyflavor@gmail.com

ABOUT THE PHOTOGRAPHER:

Sheena Jibson

If Sheena isn't behind the lens of a camera capturing her food and family adventures, you will find her on a mountain trail running with her dog, Charley. Sheena lives in Utah with her husband and two small children. "The Family Flavor" is her first book. You can also see more of Sheena's work on her blog, "In The Little Red House", at www.inthelittleredhouse.blogspot.com

Thanks A Whole Lot

This book required a lot of support and feedback from friends both near and far. I am constantly amazed by the kindness and support of so many wonderful, inspiring people. Truly, this world isn't as horrible as some may say.

Tasha Allen, Veronica Anthony, Sarah Barton, Tiffany Bednar, Kristi Brown, Vanessa Brown, Kelsey Carreon, Katie Cassady, Amanda Chase, Jean Choate, Anne Clawson, Caitlyn Cox, Julie DeCoria, Jess Efrid, Joni Gardine, Emily Gurney, Erica Grover, Elma Hall, Haley Hall, Michelle Hall, Becky Holbrook, Jaime Horton, Michelle Hunt, Rachel Jackson, Sheena Jibson, Amanda Johnson, Lindsey Johnson, Mallory Johnson, Courtney Jones, Amie Kanengeiser, Jessica Makin, Gina McGary, Marie Moser, Karla Munson, Amanda Nokelby, Stephanie Ortiz, Mistie Park, Shannon Parsons, Jack Peterson, Lauren Peterson, Sue Peterson, Jane Piotrowski, Chelsy Plowman, Windy Reay, Megan Romo, Amber Sandberg, Pat Segal, Robin Shick, Ashley Swanson, Ashley Thalman, Morgan Thomas, Kristin Townsend, Kalli Verbecky and Stephanie Younger.

Most importantly, many thanks go to my husband, Ethan. Without his support and encouragement, you wouldn't have this book in your hands.